REMEMBERING YOUR BAPTISM

"Kathryn Morales has given the church another fresh devotional to use. This time she works with baptism. The Holy Scriptures are dripping wet. So is this devotional and so is your life, if you pay attention. Morales explores the biblical allusions to baptism and then applies these promises to our lives. This is what sets apart Morales' devotionals: they are about the promise of Christ's grace delivered to sinners. Always about the promise!"

—Rev. Dr. Michael Berg,
Professor of Theology, Wisconsin Lutheran College

"*Remembering Your Baptism* is an incredibly edifying read that not only teaches but comforts. Over and over again, Kathryn finds Christ within His sacrament. Baptism is simply Jesus for sinners. In a market oversaturated with devotionals that demand we do more for Jesus, for 40 days we hear instead the gospel. Jesus does all the work, and so Baptism becomes a place where Christ's work is for you. The 8-day week layout brilliantly encourages the reader not to mark time by what has to be done but bound to God's promise of new creation which is already ours in Baptism."

—Harrison Goodman,
Content Executive, Higher Things

"Kathryn Morales has given us a wonderful reminder of the ever-present gift of Holy Baptism in these daily devotions. Centered on the truth of Holy Scripture and what it says about Christ-for-us in water and Word, this book is a fantastic addition to the reader's Lenten discipline, and can be revisited in years to come as a comfort and assurance that our Lord is always with us."

—Pr. Duane Bamsch,
Grace Lutheran Church, Grass Valley, CA,
Higher Things for Lutheran Youth

"Martin Luther once said that 'every Christian has enough in Baptism to learn and to practice all his life.' Kathy's devotional on "Remembering Your Baptism" helps with this task by taking us on a deep dive into the ocean of God's Word where we see the wonderful works and promises of God that all come together in Holy Baptism for God's people. Her book will help you 'learn and practice' what it means to be baptized as you read the wonderful Christ-centered, Scripture-soaked devotions contained in these pages!"

—**Pastor Mark Buetow,**
Zion Lutheran Church and School,
McHenry, Illinois

"Reading and spiritually digesting *Remembering Your Baptism* is an unforgettable faith-filled journey. Author Kathryn Morales really knows how to turn a phrase as she gives delightful biblical insights into the foundational reality of baptism. *Remembering Your Baptism* devotionally energizes the reader in appreciating how repentance is a return to one's baptism and true identity as a forgiven child of God. This book is the remedy for the temptation of outgrowing and leaving behind one's baptism!"

—**Joel Pless, Ph.D., Professor of Theology,**
Wisconsin Lutheran College

REMEMBERING YOUR BAPTISM

**A 40-DAY DEVOTIONAL
PART OF THE SINNER/SAINT DEVOTIONAL SERIES**

KATHRYN MORALES

Foreword by:
DONAVON RILEY

Remembering Your Baptism: A 40-Day Devotional

© 2024 New Reformation Publications

All rights reserved. No part of this publication may be reproduced, distributed, or transmitted in any form or by any means, including photocopying, recording, or other electronic or mechanical methods, without the prior written permission of the publisher, except in the case of brief quotations embodied in critical reviews and certain other noncommercial uses permitted by copyright law. For permission requests, write to the publisher at the address below.

Unless otherwise indicated, all Scripture quotations are from the ESV® Bible (The Holy Bible, English Standard Version®), © 2001 by Crossway, a publishing ministry of Good News Publishers. Used by permission. All rights reserved. The ESV text may not be quoted in any publication made available to the public by a Creative Commons license. The ESV may not be translated in whole or in part into any other language.

Published by:
1517 Publishing
PO Box 54032
Irvine, CA 92619-4032

Publisher's Cataloging-In-Publication Data
(Prepared by Cassidy Cataloguing Services, Inc.)

Names: Morales, Kathryn, author. | Riley, Donavon, writer of foreword.
    Title: Remembering your baptism : a 40-day devotional / Kathryn Morales ; foreword by Donavon Riley.
Description: Irvine, CA : 1517 Publishing, [2025] | Series: The sinner/saint devotional series | Includes bibliographical references.
Identifiers: ISBN: 978-1-964419-03-9 (paperback) | 978-1-964419-04-6 (ebook)
Subjects: LCSH: Baptism—Prayers and devotions. | Jesus Christ—Devotional literature. | Creation— Prayers and devotions. | Water—Religious aspects—Christianity. | Lutheran Church—Prayers and devotions. | Devotional exercises. | LCGFT: Devotional literature. | BISAC: RELIGION / Christian Living / Devotional. | RELIGION / Christian Rituals & Practice / Sacraments. | RELIGION / Christianity / Lutheran.
Classification: LCC: BX8073.5 .M67 2025 | DDC: 234.161—dc23

Printed in the United States of America.

Cover art by Zachariah James Stuef.

To my husband, Ryan

Contents

Foreword by: Donavon Riley — *xi*
Understanding the Unique Structure of this Devotional — *xv*

WEEK ONE

Day 1	In the Beginning (Genesis 1:1-3)	2
Day 2	A Watery Fortress (1 Peter 3:21)	6
Day 3	The Stricken Rock (1 Corinthians 10:4)	10
Day 4	Saturated Sermons (Acts 8:35)	14
Day 5	The Sign of Jonah (Jonah 1:17)	18
Day 6	Marked With the Cross (Colossians 2:17)	22
Day 7	Be Holy (Leviticus 19:1-2)	26
Day 8	Eight Days Later (John 20:26-27)	30

WEEK TWO

Day 1	Thundering Waters (Psalm 29:3)	36
Day 2	A Triumphant Flood (Exodus 15:1-2)	40
Day 3	Planted in Baptismal Waters (Psalm 1:3)	44
Day 4	Entering God's Kingdom (John 3:5-6)	48
Day 5	Absorbing Our Sin (Matthew 3:13-15)	52
Day 6	Watery Vestments (Genesis 3:21)	56
Day 7	An Extravagant Father (Luke 15:22-23)	60
Day 8	Water and the Word (John 2:7-9)	64

WEEK THREE

Day 1	A Baptismal Exorcism (Ephesians 2:1-3)	70
Day 2	Ordinary Water (2 Kings 5:14)	74
Day 3	Baptismal Hyssop (Psalm 51:7)	78
Day 4	Washing of Regeneration (Titus 3:5)	82
Day 5	Caught in the Word (Luke 5:10)	86
Day 6	Faithed (Matthew 28:19-20)	90
Day 7	Entombed in the Water (Romans 6:3-4)	94
Day 8	A New Identity (Colossians 2:11-12)	98

WEEK FOUR

Day 1	Illuminated Waters (Colossians 1:13-14)	104
Day 2	The Final Word (Luke 24:5-6)	108
Day 3	Still Waters (Psalm 23:1-3)	112
Day 4	Drowned and Raised (Matthew 14:30-31)	115
Day 5	What Debt? (Psalm 130:3-5)	119
Day 6	Splashing in Baptismal Waters (Mark 10:14)	123
Day 7	A Sanctified Bath (1 Corinthians 6:11)	127
Day 8	Called by Name (John 20:17)	131

WEEK FIVE

Day 1	Baptized into the Promised Land (Joshua 3:17)	136
Day 2	A Naval Church (Genesis 7:15-16)	140
Day 3	Parched Bones (Ezekiel 37:10)	144
Day 4	Our Great High Priest (Zechariah 3:3-4)	148
Day 5	Anointed (2 Corinthians 1:21-22)	152
Day 6	The River of Life (John 19:34)	156
Day 7	Baptismal Confidence (Acts 2:37-38)	159
Day 8	A Watery Benediction (Numbers 6:24-27)	163

Appendix   167

Foreword

There is a rhythm to baptism. Angels and archangels and the whole company of heaven singing. The Holy Spirit calling the tune, seeing his promise through to the end. And us, the Father's beloved baptized, wrestling with sin in our earthly vocations, dancing with Christ Jesus in worship.

Baptism isn't merely a sentence in the Bible: "Be baptized every one of you in the name of Jesus Christ for the forgiveness of your sins, and you shall receive the gift of the Holy Spirit. For the promise is for you and your children, and for all who are far off" (Acts 2:38-39). It's not a prison stretch that awaits heavenly pardon. It's a judgment.

We the heavy-hearted, the shattered, the spoiled leftovers of the Fall, are divinely judged. Unripeness is our personal sin. We are more akin to the wolf than to the Shepherd. We don't get an easy ride in the Bible. So we trudge to the font, time to take our lickings. Then, the judgement, the water, the words, the wild dove descending upon us. Forgiveness! Life! Eternal Salvation!

Baptism is a return to the genesis of our beginnings.

On the seventh day, God rested in his temple. On the seventh day, Jesus rested. But on the eighth day, Jesus was raised from death. Why? The eighth day symbolizes eternity. Baptism is an eighth day event, an eternity of judgment that declares us free from sin, death, and hell's blight. But, on this side of the resurrection, we must still abide by the demands of the clock, its ticks, ticks, ticks a constant reminder that Jesus has not returned quite yet. So for six days we labor, and on the seventh day we rest, all while living by faith in the eighth day, our baptismal day, new life day.

That is the theme of this book. Kathryn Morales has written a forty-day devotional composed of five eight-day weeks, resulting in a book that engages readers with God's word and works from the first day of the week, when God separated the light from the darkness and Mary Magdalene came to the tomb, to the seventh day, when God rested in a tomb, his holy temple, not stopping until she's led us safely to the eight day, eternal hope and joy. Jesus breaks the pattern of the seven-day week so why shouldn't we, especially in our daily devotions?

On the eighth day we can revel in a cosmos of meaning. The edges, ditches, moats, and boundaries are removed. Now it's all watering holes and sacred mountains for those who are baptized into Christ Jesus. The wall of thorns is cleared away. The gates of Paradise are open. The Tree of Life produces low hanging fruit for us to eat. Our Savior will have his way with us now, at his pace, carried along by currents of grace and mercy.

That's our life now. Watery-eyed, wetly clothed. Eighth-day ecstasy. What happens next, we may not imagine. But, in what follows, the author uses the words of Scripture to paint a glorious picture of baptismal life. The Bible describes it as beautiful, tender, urgent, bloody, sometimes quiet, sometimes stumbling, but always thrilling. And yet, at the same time, every biblical narrative, each day's reading, focuses our attention on the same truth: "Baptism now saves you" (1 Peter 3:21).

This book is for our comfort, for encouragement amid daily struggles, when we're taking our lumps, looking to slake our thirst around a dry lakebed. When the storms of life mock us, this devotional is an invitation to flee to the temple of our Lord for rest, and to be rejuvenated.

So turn off your phone, take a deep breath, and remember your baptism. Fall into the arms of your heavenly Father and read Scripture with Kathy Morales and reflect on how baptism, through simple water and God's dazzling Word, daily drowns and washes you into newness of life in Christ Jesus.

Donavon Riley

Understanding the Unique Structure of this Devotional

NOW ON THE FIRST DAY OF THE WEEK MARY MAGDALENE CAME TO THE TOMB EARLY, WHILE IT WAS STILL DARK, AND SAW THAT THE STONE HAD BEEN TAKEN AWAY FROM THE TOMB.

—John 20:1

The act of creation took place over six days, culminating in God resting from his work on the seventh. This fundamental seven-day structure underlies our understanding of weeks.

However, this devotional's unique structure sets it apart from traditional seven-day weeks. Instead of a typical week, this baptismal devotional is composed of five eight-day weeks, resulting in a forty-day devotional.

The Rhythm of Resurrection: Why Eight-Day Weeks?

The church has long observed that in his resurrection, Jesus breaks the pattern of the seven-day week. After he has completed his work of our salvation on the sixth day of Good Friday, he rests from his labors on the Sabbath, the seventh day. It is on the first day of the week, that new eighth-day, in which his resurrection from the dead takes place. This devotional is composed of eight-day weeks to reflect on this eighth day of resurrection. It's that salvific connection between Jesus' resurrection and our own baptism which highlights the significance of an eighth day.

Safe in the Baptismal Ark: Why Five Weeks?

Through baptism, we are born again and brought into this eighth day. We are saved, as the eight souls on the ark were saved, through water and God's promise. The apostle Peter writes in his epistle, "God's patience waited in the days of Noah, while the ark was being prepared, in which a few, that is, eight persons, were brought safely through water. Baptism, which corresponds to this, now saves you" (1 Pet 3:20-21).

As those eight saints were kept safe in the ark for forty days and forty nights, so too are we kept safe in Christ, our ark. This devotional is composed of five, eight-day weeks to reflect on these forty days of the flood.

Approaches to Reading

Considering the rhythm of our seven-day weeks, however, there are three approaches for delving into this devotional.

The first is to read the devotional within the five-week layout. The seventh day may be read in the morning of the corresponding day and the eighth day may be read on the evening of the same. This would result in reading two devotionals on the seventh day.

The second approach would be to read one devotional a day, disregarding the weeks, resulting in a forty-day devotional.

The third approach is to be free in your baptismal life and read this at your own pace. Take time to read Scripture and reflect on how baptism, through the water and Word, daily drowns and washes you into newness of life in Christ.

WEEK ONE

In the Beginning

THE FIRST DAY OF THE FIRST WEEK

IN THE BEGINNING, GOD CREATED THE HEAVENS AND THE EARTH. THE EARTH WAS WITHOUT FORM AND VOID, AND DARKNESS WAS OVER THE FACE OF THE DEEP. AND THE SPIRIT OF GOD WAS HOVERING OVER THE FACE OF THE WATERS. AND GOD SAID, "LET THERE BE LIGHT," AND THERE WAS LIGHT.

—*Genesis 1:1-3*

In the beginning there was water and God's word. As the Spirit hovered over the waters, the Father sent forth his Word into the formless void, and said, "Let there be light," and there was light. God's Word has the power to bring forth what it proclaims.

In the opening of his Gospel account, the apostle John writes that this Word of God which created all things is Jesus. John mirrors the beginning of Genesis as he writes.

> In the beginning was the Word, and the Word was with God, and the Word was God. He was in the beginning with God. All things were made through him, and without him was not any thing made that was made. In him was life, and the life was the light of men. (John 1:1-4)

In the beginning, Jesus was there with the Father and the Spirit creating all things for us. In his epistle, the apostle Peter states, "the earth was formed out of water and through water by the word of God" (2 Pet 3:5).

The Spirit who hovered over the waters at creation, hovers over the waters of our baptism. The Father who sent out his Word into the formless void and said, "Let there be light," sends his Word into the formless void of our hearts as we are baptized in the name of the Father, Son, and Holy Spirit. The apostle Paul writes, "For God, who said, 'Let light shine out of darkness,' has shone in our hearts to give the light of the knowledge of the glory of God in the face of Jesus Christ" (2 Cor 4:6).

Baptism is greater than merely being a symbol. Baptism is a promise. It is a promise that through water and God's word we are re-created. We are united to Christ and given new life in him. Our sins are forgiven, and we have been made children of God. Through water and the word, the work of Jesus is delivered to us.

God's word has the power to bring forth what it proclaims in baptism. The prophet Isaiah writes, "So shall my word be that goes out from my mouth; it shall not return to me empty, but it shall accomplish that which I purpose, and shall succeed in the thing for which I sent it." (Isa 55:11)

Baptism is a promise dependent on Christ's work for us and God's promise to us through water and the word. Despite our sin, God's word accomplishes its purpose for our salvation. We can be certain of our salvation because we are baptized.

With ordinary water connected with his efficacious word, God creates faith. He sustains this baptismal faith through the Holy Spirit given to us in baptism.[1] The early church father, Tertullian, beautifully connects the working of the Spirit in baptism with the Spirit in creation when he writes, "The Spirit of God, who hovered over (the waters) from the beginning, would continue to linger over the waters of the baptized."[2]

The Trinity who created all things has graciously re-created us in Christ through the gift of baptism. We have been marked and named as belonging to the Father, Son, and Holy Spirit. This external word placed upon us in baptism assures us that our sins are forgiven, we are children of God, and we will rise with Christ, our Lord, in the resurrection. Sin, death, and the devil have no power over us, they can no longer accuse us, we are baptized into Christ!

---

[1] Titus 3:5-6.
[2] Tertullian, *On Baptism* (Savage, MN: Lighthouse Christian Publishing, 2015), 8.

Heavenly Father, through your word you created all things. We give you thanks that through water and your word in Holy Baptism, you have created new life in us through your Son. Graciously keep us in your baptized family, that we may daily die to sin and rise to the new life you have given us in Christ, that we may love and serve our neighbors. Amen.

> **FOR FURTHER REFLECTION, READ JOHN 1:1-18.**

THE SECOND DAY OF THE FIRST WEEK

A Watery Fortress

BAPTISM, WHICH CORRESPONDS TO THIS, NOW SAVES YOU, NOT AS A REMOVAL OF DIRT FROM THE BODY BUT AS AN APPEAL TO GOD FOR A GOOD CONSCIENCE, THROUGH THE RESURRECTION OF JESUS CHRIST.

—1 Peter 3:21

The vessel the carpenter had built with his own hands withstood the waters of God's judgment. For forty days and forty nights, the earth drowned in the rains of God's judgment. The wickedness of the earth was swallowed up in the waves of a watery death.

Noah had built this ark of salvation at the Lord's command. As the storm raged around the ark, Noah's family of eight, who had taken refuge inside its gopher wood embrace remained safe. The floodwaters that brought death to every living thing on earth were the same waters that upheld this congregation of eight.

After forty days and forty nights the floodwaters lifted this ark of faith high above the earth. The Lord had blotted out sinful mankind and all living things in the floodwaters below this floating church. All that remained was Noah, his family and all living creatures on the ark.

The Lord remembered his promise to his saints and sent a wind to dry up the floodwaters. As the waters began to subside, the ark came to rest on a mountain. In time, as the waters receded and vegetation appeared, a dove sent by Noah returned with a fresh olive leaf.

In his first epistle, the apostle Peter draws a straight line between this account of the flood in Genesis to baptism. This account in Genesis is saturated with baptismal imagery. The floodwaters that brought death to a sinful world and life to those sheltered in the ark illustrate the true saving power of Christ in baptism.

Jesus is our greater Noah. He is sent by God to prepare for us a refuge from the storm. Our carpenter builds for us a watery fortress with his own nail pierced hands. As God's judgment for our sin rested on Mount Calvary, water flowed from the side of our watery refuge.[3] We remain safe from God's righteous judgment within the ark of Christ.

---

[3] John 19:34.

Jesus took the fullness of God's wrath for our sin, and we, who reside in Christ, are saved from those waves of judgment. Our deliverance comes by water connected with God's word.

Just as Noah found favor with God, we also find peace and favor through the work of Christ for us. Baptism now saves you, writes Peter, "not as a removal of dirt from the body but as an appeal to God for a good conscience, through the resurrection of Jesus Christ" (1 Peter 3:21).

In the watery grave of baptism, our Old Adam is drowned and dies. Just as the Lord blotted out every living thing from the earth, so too he blots out our sins. They are no more. Our transgressions were swallowed up in Christ's death and buried in his tomb. The Lord says, "I, I am he who blots out your transgressions for my own sake, and I will not remember your sins" (Isa 43:25).

Baptism now saves us, but not because of any work on our part. Peter can speak of the saving work of baptism because it is solely the work of Father, Son, and Holy Spirit for us.

The waves of God's judgment cannot harm us in Christ. We are carried on the waves of baptism, cradled by the ark of Christ Himself to the shores of the resurrection.

The Holy Spirit is given as an assurance of our new life in Christ. Just as the dove brought back a fresh olive leaf to Noah, confirming that new life had emerged from death, so the Holy

Spirit, like the dove, reassures us with the promise of eternal life in Christ our Lord.

As we remember our baptism, we remember the God who remembers us. In the merciful God in whom Noah found favor, we too find favor through the work of Christ. Our sins are washed away in the floodwaters of baptism. Our transgressions are blotted out as we remain secure in the watery fortress of Christ. Through the gift of the Holy Spirit, we have the assurance that in Christ, we have received eternal life through his death for us.

Heavenly Father, through your word you created all things. We give you thanks that through water and your word in Holy Baptism, you have created new life in us through your Son. Graciously keep us in your baptized family, that we may daily die to sin and rise to the new life you have given us in Christ, that we may love and serve our neighbors. Amen.

> **FOR FURTHER REFLECTION, READ GENESIS 8:1-19.**

THE THIRD DAY OF THE FIRST WEEK

The Stricken Rock

FOR THEY DRANK FROM THE SPIRITUAL ROCK THAT FOLLOWED THEM, AND THE ROCK WAS CHRIST.

—1 Corinthians 10:4

The Old Testament overflows with baptismal imagery. Christ is continually present in the midst of his people even before his incarnation. The gospel-soaked texts of the Old Testament foreshadow Christ's work for sinners.

The apostle Paul takes his readers on a journey back to the wilderness of Sinai. In his first letter to the church in Corinth, Paul revisits the gospel-soaked book of Exodus. Throughout this Old Testament book, God continues, time and again, to preserve his people.

The Lord brought his people out of the land of Egypt, freeing them from their slavery. As the streets ran red with doorposts painted with the blood of a lamb, the Lord's promise to pass over those marked with the blood of the lamb, spared the lives of their firstborn.[4]

The Lord fought for his people as he parted the waters of the Red Sea, bringing Israel safely through the crossing on dry ground. As their captors followed, the Lord collapsed the waters of the Red Sea onto the armies of Pharaoh, swallowing them in water.

The Lord always provided and fought for his people, however, they continually grumbled against him. Yet, the Lord was merciful. Where Israel lacked water, the Lord miraculously made bitter water sweet to drink.[5] When rumbling stomachs came to Moses, the Lord rained down bread from heaven.[6]

Throughout the book of Exodus, one thing becomes clear. Even in the midst of their grumbling unbelief, the Lord always provided.

The apostle Paul picks up the account in Exodus where the Israelites again find themselves without water. Instead of looking to the Lord to provide, they again protested against Moses. As Moses, frustrated with God's people, cried out, "What shall I do with this people?" (Exod 17:4), the Lord responded, "you shall strike the rock, and water shall come out of it, and the people will drink" (Exod 17:6).

---

[4] Exodus 12:7.
[5] Exodus 15:25.
[6] Exodus 16:4.

Moses did as the Lord commanded and out of the stricken rock flowed life-giving water. Paul says, "The Rock was Christ" (1 Cor 10:4).

Just as the Lord provided for his people from the side of the stricken rock, so too we receive life from the pierced side of our Rock, Christ.[7] Through this Rock comes the life-imparting waters of Holy Baptism.

The Lord provides, even in the midst of our grumbling unbelief. Just as the apostle Paul stated that this Rock followed the children of Israel, so too our Rock has promised to abide with us.[8] The hymnist George Bourne beautifully draws on this imagery as he writes,

> *Life imparting heav'nly manna, Stricken rock with streaming side, Heav'n and earth with loud hosanna, Worship You, the Lamb who died.*[9]

Our stricken rock gives us life through water and the Word. He gives to us the heavenly manna of his very body and blood.[10] In these gifts, Jesus, our stricken Rock, forgives our sins and promises us everlasting life with himself.

---

[7] John 19:34
[8] Matthew 28:20.
[9] George Bourne, "Hymn 534," in *Lutheran Service Book: Pew Edition* (Saint Louis, MO: Concordia Publishing House, 2006), 534.
[10] John 6:32- 35.

Heavenly Father, through your word you created all things. We give you thanks that through water and your word in Holy Baptism, you have created new life in us through your Son. Graciously keep us in your baptized family, that we may daily die to sin and rise to the new life you have given us in Christ, that we may love and serve our neighbors. Amen.

> **FOR FURTHER REFLECTION, READ EXODUS 17:1-7.**

Saturated Sermons

THE FOURTH DAY OF THE FIRST WEEK

THEN PHILIP OPENED HIS MOUTH,
AND BEGINNING WITH THIS SCRIPTURE HE
TOLD HIM THE GOOD NEWS ABOUT JESUS.

—Acts 8:35

Philip's question interrupted the Ethiopian's perplexing contemplation. The Ethiopian was traveling home from Jerusalem as he sat in his chariot, reading from the prophet Isaiah. But the words of the prophet fell flat. Being sent to the Ethiopian by the Holy Spirit, Philip asked him, "Do you understand what you are reading?" The Ethiopian responded to Philip's inquiry, "How can I, unless someone guides me?" (Acts 8:30-31).

Philip's inquiry led to an invitation by the Ethiopian to join him and delve into the prophet Isaiah's words. Together, they read from the prophet Isaiah,

Like a lamb that is led to the slaughter, and like a sheep that before its shearers is silent, so he opened not his mouth. By oppression and judgment he was taken away; and as for his generation, who considered that he was cut off out of the land of the living (Isa 53:7-8).

The Ethiopian, a gentile and outsider of the Jewish faith and Scriptures, asked Philip, "About whom, I ask you, does the prophet say this, about himself or about someone else?" (Acts 8:34). Philip proceeded by taking the Ethiopian straight to Jesus, beginning with this reading from the prophet Isaiah.

Philip, sent by the Holy Spirit to the Ethiopian, declared the good news about Jesus for him. He didn't just explain the Scriptures to the Ethiopian. Phillip showed him how all of it pointed to Jesus.

Philip knew the Scriptures. But, more importantly, through the gift of the Holy Spirit, he knew *who* the Scriptures were about. One of the first recorded interactions with Philip is in John's Gospel. Upon being called by Jesus, Philip found his friend Nathanael and was ecstatic to bring him to Jesus. He said, "We have found him of whom Moses and the Law and also the prophets wrote, Jesus of Nazareth, the son of Joseph" (John 1:45). Philip brought his friend Nathanael to Jesus, just as he brought the Ethiopian to Jesus. By the working of the Holy Spirit, Philip was continually bringing those he encountered to Jesus.

As the Scriptures were opened to the Ethiopian, revealing the saving work of Jesus for him, they came across some water in their travels back to Africa. The Ethiopian exclaimed, "See, here is water! What prevents me from being baptized?" (Acts 8:37).

The good news about Jesus led the Ethiopian straight to the waters of baptism. Philip's sermon on Isaiah was saturated with the work of Jesus. As the Ethiopians' eyes were opened by the faithful preaching and working of the Holy Spirit, he was led to the waters of baptism to receive the very Jesus who had been preached to him. He was led to the waters of baptism in which all the promises of Jesus would be delivered to him.

Through the work of the Holy Spirit, we too are brought to the waters of Holy Baptism. Just as the Holy Spirit sent Philip to proclaim the gospel to the Ethiopian, so too he sends us faithful pastors to proclaim the good news of Jesus and his work for us. Through this proclamation, God's word creates and sustains faith in the work of Christ for us.

As baptized children of God, we are continually pointed back to our baptism. The work of Christ was personally delivered as we were baptized in the name of the Father, Son, and Holy Spirit. We have been promised the forgiveness of all our sins, past, present, and future, through this gift of baptism. In the proclamation of the gospel, our eyes are continually directed back to the baptismal font where our Lord has claimed us as his own.

Heavenly Father, through your word you created all things. We give you thanks that through water and your word in Holy Baptism, you have created new life in us through your Son. Graciously keep us in your baptized family, that we may daily die to sin and rise to the new life you have given us in Christ, that we may love and serve our neighbors. Amen.

> **FOR FURTHER REFLECTION, READ ACTS 8:26-40.**

THE FIFTH DAY OF THE FIRST WEEK

The Sign of Jonah

AND THE LORD APPOINTED A GREAT FISH TO SWALLOW UP JONAH. AND JONAH WAS IN THE BELLY OF THE FISH THREE DAYS AND THREE NIGHTS.

—Jonah 1:17

The word of the Lord came to Jonah and said, "Arise, go to Nineveh, that great city, and call out against it, for their evil has come up before me" (Jonah 1:2). So, Jonah rose up. He knew full well of God's mercy. Jonah confessed, "I knew that you are a gracious God and merciful, slow to anger and abounding in steadfast love, and relenting from disaster" (Jonah 4:2). And that's why he's not going.

Jonah refused to go to the far country of Nineveh. He refused to preach to people who engage in reckless, sinful, and wild living. Jonah refused to go to Nineveh, the capital of Syria, the enemy of his people, Israel. Instead of setting out towards Nineveh as the Lord commanded, Jonah set sail to Tarshish, as far away from Nineveh as he could go.

As God's rebellious and defiant prophet set sail to Tarshish, the Lord went with him. The psalmist, King David wrote, "Where shall I go from your Spirit? Or where shall I flee from your presence? If I ascend to heaven, you are there! If I make my bed in Sheol, you are there!" (Ps 139:7-8). Jonah cannot flee the Lord's presence. If Jonah went to Nineveh, the Lord would be there. If he fled to Tarshish, the Lord would be there.

In his mercy, the Lord sent a storm upon the Mediterranean Sea where Jonah was traveling. After confessing his sin to the crew, he asked to be thrown overboard. As he was thrown into the sea, the sea was immediately calmed. The sailors were spared. As for Jonah, a great fish was sent to swallow up God's runaway prophet for three days and three nights in the watery depths of the sea.

As Jonah sat in the watery depths of the sea, he called out to the Lord from his grave within the belly of a fish. The Lord is merciful to Jonah and on the third day, Jonah is resurrected as the fish spits him out onto dry land.

When Jesus was asked for a sign by the scribes and Pharisees, he answered them, "an evil and adulterous generation seeks for a sign, but no sign will be given to it except the sign of the prophet Jonah. For just as Jonah was three days and three nights in the belly of the great fish, so will the Son of Man be three days and three nights in the heart of the earth" (Matt 12:39-40).

Of all the prophets in the Old Testament, Jesus points to Jonah as the sign they will receive. Jonah, the prophet who was sent to preach to the enemies of Israel, who was buried in the belly of the fish, and was resurrected on the third day, is the sign they will be given. Jesus declared to them, "behold, something greater than Jonah is here" (Matt 12:41).

The book of Jonah illustrates the mercy and abounding steadfast love of our God who pursues his enemies. He will have his prophet preach to the city of Nineveh in order that they may repent and be shown mercy. The Lord, who is slow to anger and abounding in steadfast love, shows mercy to Jonah, the runaway prophet, and to us.

Jesus is our greater Jonah. Though Jesus was without sin, he was made to be our sin and was thrown into the sea of God's wrath and judgment for us.[11] The prophet Micah writes, "He will again have compassion on us; he will tread our iniquities underfoot. You will cast all our sins into the depths of the sea" (Mic 7:19). We have been spared from the punishment for our sin as Jesus was swallowed up in death for us. Just as Jonah burst from his watery grave on the third day, so too Jesus is raised on the third day.

Just as Jonah was saved by the fish who had been appointed to swallow him up and spare his life, so also have we been swallowed up by our greater fish in the waters of baptism. In

---

[11] 2 Corinthians 5:21.

the water and the word of baptism, we are swallowed up in the name of the Father, Son, and Holy Spirit as we are kept safe in Christ, our fish.

Our Lord called us by name and pursued us in the waters of our baptism. He has cast our sins into the depths of the sea, and we are saved from the storm of God's righteous judgment for our sins. God saves us in our great fish, Jesus, and on the last day, we too will be spit out of the grave into life everlasting.

Heavenly Father, through your word you created all things. We give you thanks that through water and your word in Holy Baptism, you have created new life in us through your Son. Graciously keep us in your baptized family, that we may daily die to sin and rise to the new life you have given us in Christ, that we may love and serve our neighbors. Amen.

> **FOR FURTHER REFLECTION, READ LUKE 15:11-32.**

THE SIXTH DAY OF THE FIRST WEEK

Marked With the Cross

THESE ARE A SHADOW OF THE THINGS TO COME, BUT THE SUBSTANCE BELONGS TO CHRIST.

—Colossians 2:17

Many of the historic feast and festival days celebrated in the Old Testament are flooded with the narratives of God's faithful deliverance and mercy. In these celebrations, God's people looked back on God's promises, and the fulfillment of those promises. The Passover, which was celebrated yearly, is one such account.

The narrative of the Passover begins in Exodus, the second book of the Old Testament. In this book is written the account of God's deliverance of his people who had been held as slaves in Egypt for four hundred years. God remembered his people and led them out of their captivity and into a new land. Through his servant Moses, the Lord performed wonders and sent plagues upon the Egyptians, their captors. The culmination of this deliverance came with the Passover.

As the final plague the Lord brings upon the land of Egypt the death of the firstborn. The Lord was to pass over the land of Egypt around midnight and the firstborn of the people of Egypt and their livestock would die. This Passover of the Lord was one of judgment.

The Passover was also one of deliverance. At God's institution and by his command, each household in Israel took a lamb without blemish and killed the lamb at twilight. The blood of the lamb was then painted on the doorposts of the household and the lamb was eaten as part of the Passover meal.

At the center of the Passover was a lamb and a promise. The Lord promised, "when I see the blood, I will pass over you, and no plague will befall you to destroy you, when I strike the land of Egypt" (Exod 12:13). The blood of the lamb painted on their doorposts, saved them from the judgment of God upon the land of Egypt.

In his letter to the Colossians, Paul speaks of the Old Testament festivals and laws, such as the Passover, as shadows now brought to completion in Christ. All of Scripture finds its fulfillment in Christ.

At the center of baptism is a Lamb and a promise. At our Lord's institution, and by his command, all nations are to be baptized in the name of the Father and of the Son and of the Holy Spirit.[12] Baptism is a sacrament of deliverance.

Just as the center of Passover was the lamb without blemish, so too baptism centers around the Lamb of God, who marks us and covers us with his holy and precious blood. As we are baptized, the Lord's judgment for our sin passes over us and falls on the Lamb who gave himself for us. The firstborn, the only Son of God dies in our place.

Traditionally, in the service of Holy Baptism, the sign of the cross is made on the head and heart of the baptized. The baptized is marked as one claimed by Christ in baptism, buried with him, and raised with him.[13] Through water and the word, we are delivered from our captors of sin, death, and the devil.

The theologian John Kleinig explains how we can daily remember our baptism in this way,

> We therefore live our whole life under the sign of the cross. As we get up each morning, we, in a small way, share in the resurrection of Jesus; as we go to bed each evening, we share in His death.[14]

Each day we remember our exodus, our baptism. It is a daily Passover in which God passes over our sins as he has placed

---

[12] Matthew 28:19.
[13] Romans 6:4.
[14] John W. Kleinig, *Grace Upon Grace: Spirituality for Today* (Saint Louis: Concordia Publishing House, 2008), 79.

them on Jesus, our Paschal Lamb. We are marked with the forgiveness, righteousness, and life of our Lord, who has redeemed us. We can make the sign of the cross and proclaim, "I am baptized!"

Heavenly Father, through your word you created all things. We give you thanks that through water and your word in Holy Baptism, you have created new life in us through your Son. Graciously keep us in your baptized family, that we may daily die to sin and rise to the new life you have given us in Christ, that we may love and serve our neighbors. Amen.

> **FOR FURTHER REFLECTION, READ EXODUS 12:1-28.**

THE SEVENTH DAY OF THE FIRST WEEK

Be Holy

AND THE LORD SPOKE TO MOSES, SAYING, "SPEAK TO ALL THE CONGREGATION OF THE PEOPLE OF ISRAEL AND SAY TO THEM, 'YOU SHALL BE HOLY, FOR I THE LORD YOUR GOD AM HOLY.'"

—Leviticus 19:1-2

From the account of creation at the beginning of Genesis, to the patriarchs, judges, kings, and prophets, the Old Testament is packed with grand narratives. And then, there's Leviticus.

In Genesis, we ride the waves of the flood in the ark with Noah and his family and gaze up at the stars with Abraham. We follow the lineage of Jesus from the first promise in the garden through the patriarchs such as Abraham, Issac, and Jacob.

Then, in the second book, Exodus, we follow the majestic rescue of God's people out of their enslavement in Egypt.

God parts the Red Sea and brings his people out from their captivity on dry ground.

And then, there's Leviticus.

Instead of a book filled with exciting wonders and miracles, Leviticus is a book filled with ordinances and worship instructions for God's people. This third book of the Old Testament, however, is a storehouse of God's promises to his people. The Gospel of Leviticus lays out a blueprint foreshadowing what the Lamb of God, our great High Priest, will accomplish for us.

Throughout the book of Leviticus, God instructs his people on holiness. The pages of Leviticus are filled with the weight of God's holiness. The Lord instructs Moses to tell the congregation of Israel, "You shall be holy, for I the LORD your God am holy" (Lev 19:2).

Israel was to be holy, as the Lord their God was holy. Israel's holiness didn't come from their efforts. It came as a gift of God. Holiness belongs to God alone, and he graciously shares it with his people.

In the book of Leviticus, the Lord is making a promise to his people. God's people shall be holy, as he is holy. And, if they are to be holy as he is holy, he must be the one to make them holy. Jesus, our great High Priest will be the one to make us holy as he is holy.

And what does it mean to be holy? The apostle Paul writes in his address to the saints in Corinth, "To the church of God that is in Corinth, to those sanctified in Christ Jesus" (1 Cor 1:2). To be holy is to be sanctified, or set apart, in Christ Jesus. But how does this happen? How does God fulfill his promise to make his people holy, to make us holy, as he is holy?

He does this through the water and his word of Holy Baptism.

Through water and the word in baptism, our Lord sanctifies us, making us holy by placing his holy name upon us. He says, "I am the LORD your God" (Lev 18:30). We are made holy in the waters of baptism because there, we are connected to Christ Jesus, our Lord.

Just as Israel could only receive holiness from the Lord, so too we can only receive holiness from the Lord. We receive this holiness as a gift through Holy Baptism. Through water and God's Word, the Lord puts to death our rebellious sinful nature, and gifts us with his holiness, his life.

Throughout the book of Leviticus, the Lord shows his people how they are to receive this holiness from himself through the pattern laid out for worship. Today in the Divine Service, God continues to come to us to give his holiness to us. God gifts us his holiness abundantly through the preaching of the gospel, the sacrament of the Lord's Supper, the absolution, and our baptism.

Through baptism, we are washed, sanctified, and made holy in the name of the Father, Son, and Holy Spirit. As we hear the declaration of the absolution, we receive the comfort of the forgiveness of all our sins. In the Lord's Supper we receive the very body and blood of Jesus, as he graciously pours out his life, his holiness, for us.

We are holy as the Lord our God is holy because he has made us holy and bound himself to us in baptism by his almighty Word.

Heavenly Father, through your word you created all things. We give you thanks that through water and your word in Holy Baptism, you have created new life in us through your Son. Graciously keep us in your baptized family, that we may daily die to sin and rise to the new life you have given us in Christ, that we may love and serve our neighbors. Amen.

> **FOR FURTHER REFLECTION, READ JOHN 15:1-17.**

THE EIGHTH DAY OF THE FIRST WEEK

Eight Days Later

EIGHT DAYS LATER, HIS DISCIPLES WERE INSIDE AGAIN, AND THOMAS WAS WITH THEM. ALTHOUGH THE DOORS WERE LOCKED, JESUS CAME AND STOOD AMONG THEM AND SAID, "PEACE BE WITH YOU." THEN HE SAID TO THOMAS, "PUT YOUR FINGER HERE, AND SEE MY HANDS; AND PUT OUT YOUR HAND, AND PLACE IT IN MY SIDE. DO NOT DISBELIEVE, BUT BELIEVE."

—John 20:26-27

It had been eight days since all the disciples beheld their risen Lord. Eight days since the Lord stood among them and said, "Peace be with you" (John 20:21). Eight days had passed since their eyes, ears, and all their senses, grabbed hold of their risen and glorified Lord. That is, all except Thomas.

Thomas was not with the other disciples when Jesus visited them. It had been over a week since he had seen Jesus and celebrated the Passover with him. Since then, his beloved teacher, his Lord, had been crucified, buried, and laid in a tomb. Yet, the other disciples proclaimed the good news to Thomas: they had seen Jesus! All, with the exception of Thomas, had been in the joyful presence of their resurrected Lord.

Thomas' voice resonated with sorrow, "Unless I see in his hands the mark of the nails, and place my finger into the mark of the nails, and place my hand into his side, I will never believe" (John 20:25). And Thomas was right. He would not believe. That is, Thomas cannot by his own reason and strength believe apart from the working of the Holy Spirit—nor can we.

But, on the eighth day Jesus came to Thomas.

The eighth day is not insignificant. The Scriptures are full of the language of the eighth day. God's covenant with Abraham regarding circumcision was to happen on the eighth day after birth.[15] It was on the eighth day, as the Gospel writer Luke informs us, that Jesus was taken to the temple to fulfill this covenant of circumcision and was also named.[16] It was also on the eighth day in which our Lord stepped out of his tomb, having crushed the ancient serpent's head and defeated death.

But Thomas was not there. He was not there when Jesus took his first breath that first Easter morning. He was not there to

---

[15] Genesis 17:12.
[16] Luke 2:21.

hear the angel proclaim, "Why do you seek the living among the dead? He is not here, but has risen" (Luke 24:5-6). Thomas was not in that locked room when Jesus appeared to the other disciples.

In the midst of his firm unbelief, Jesus comes to Thomas. Jesus comes not to scold Thomas into believing. He comes to gift Thomas the faith he lacks. He comes to faith Thomas. Jesus comes to comfort Thomas with the promise of sins forgiven and life everlasting. Jesus bids Thomas, "Put your finger here, and see my hands" (John 20:27). The hands which were bloodied and nailed to the cross still bear the marks but are glorified in the resurrected Christ as he reaches out and comforts his beloved disciple.

Like Thomas, we were not there. We were not there when Jesus took his first breath that first Easter morning. We were not there to hear the angel's proclamation. We were not there when Jesus came to his unbelieving disciples. We have not touched our Lord's nail-scarred hands to hear him say, "Do not disbelieve, but believe" (John 20:27).

Our Lord comes to us in a different way than he came to his apostles, to Thomas, and to the women at the tomb. Our Lord comes to us when the water is poured over us and the word is proclaimed, "I baptize you in the name of the Father, and of the Son, and of the Holy Spirit." It is there at the font where the Lord reaches out and says, "do not disbelieve, but believe." It is there at the font where the Holy Spirit works faith that clings to Christ, granting the gifts of forgiveness of sins and life everlasting. There at the baptismal font, our Lord reaches out and grabs hold of us in our unbelief.

The reformer Martin Luther wrote, "To be baptized in God's name is to be baptized not by men but by God himself. Although it is performed by men's hands, it is nevertheless truly God's own act."[17] Our Lord reaches out to us in the waters of baptism and says, "do not disbelieve, but believe." Our Lord who makes us his own in baptism gives us his Holy Spirit to sustain this gift of faith created at the font.

Heavenly Father, through your word you created all things. We give you thanks that through water and your word in Holy Baptism, you have created new life in us through your Son. Graciously keep us in your baptized family, that we may daily die to sin and rise to the new life you have given us in Christ, that we may love and serve our neighbors. Amen.

> **FOR FURTHER REFLECTION, READ JOHN 20:1-31.**

---

[17] LC IV 10.

WEEK TWO

THE FIRST DAY OF THE SECOND WEEK

Thundering Waters

THE VOICE OF THE LORD IS OVER
THE WATERS; THE GOD OF GLORY THUNDERS,
THE LORD, OVER MANY WATERS.

—Psalm 29:3

As Israel gathered at the foot of Mount Sinai, the ground began to shake as the mountain came to life trembling before the Lord of hosts. The Lord hid his voice in a loud clap of thunder. The mountain was enveloped in smoke as the Lord descended on it in the fire.[18]

As Israel wandered the desert of Sinai for forty years, the Lord placed himself in the tabernacle and lived among his people. The tabernacle was filled with the glory of the Lord.[19] God revealed himself to his people at a particular time, place, and by specific means.

---

[18] Exodus 19:18-19.
[19] Exodus 40:35.

As the apostle John begins his Gospel account, he writes, "And the Word became flesh and dwelt among us, and we have seen his glory, glory as of the only Son from the Father, full of grace and truth" (John 1:14).

The Word of God, writes John, tabernacled or dwelt among us. Just as the glory of the Lord filled the tabernacle in the wilderness as he lived among his people, so too his glory filled the manger in Bethlehem. This time, God's voice was not hidden in a thunderous clap, but in the tender cries of a newborn baby.

In his baptism, Jesus, the Word of God, was placed into the waters of baptism for us. As John baptized Jesus in the Jordan River, Jesus, the Word of God, soaked up our sins as his own. As Jesus was baptized, a voice from heaven said, "This is my beloved Son, with whom I am well pleased" (Matt 3:17).

The Word of God that made mountains tremble, placed himself upon the tree of the cross for us. This time, on the mountain of Calvary, the voice of the Lord was not in the majestic thunderous clap, but in the cry of our crucified Lord, "It is finished" (John 19:30). The glory of the Lord filled this mountain as Jesus gave himself for our sins.

As Jesus, the Word of God, breathed his last, "the earth shook, and the rocks were split" (Matt 27:51). The earth again trembled before the Lord of hosts as he was given into death for our iniquities.

Three days later, the earth shook once again as an angel rolled back the stone from the empty tomb of the resurrected Word.[20] God's Word accomplished the purpose for which it was sent, our salvation.

The Lord now places his glorious Word in the waters of baptism *for us*. The psalmist writes, "the voice of the LORD is over the waters; the God of glory thunders, the LORD, over many waters" (Ps 29:3). The God of glory thunders over the waters of our baptism as we are forgiven and marked with the name of the Father, Son, and Holy Spirit.

In the waters of baptism our sinful nature is put to death, and we are made new creations in Christ. The psalmist continues in Psalm 29 to describe God's voice as having the authority to kill and make alive. The psalmist writes, "The voice of the LORD makes the deer give birth and strips the forests bare" (Ps 29:9). Through water and God's word, we are drowned and raised in our baptism.

The Word of God has located himself in these baptismal waters to dwell or tabernacle with us, his baptized saints. As we are daily repented and brought back to the work of Christ for us in our baptism, we behold the Lamb of God who has placed himself in the waters of our baptism to take away our sin. The Word that said, "Peace! Be still!" (Mark 4:39), quiets our sin-troubled conscience with the promise of complete peace with God and life everlasting.

---

[20] Matthew 28:2.

Heavenly Father, you have washed us from our sins in Holy Baptism. You have placed your holy name upon us and made us your own dear children. Send your Holy Spirit to comfort us with the promises you have given us in baptism. Daily repent us, that we may die to sin and live in the forgiveness won for us by your Son's death and resurrection for us. Amen.

> **FOR FURTHER REFLECTION, READ PSALM 29.**

THE SECOND DAY OF THE SECOND WEEK

A Triumphant Flood

THEN MOSES AND THE PEOPLE OF ISRAEL SANG THIS SONG TO THE LORD SAYING, "I WILL SING TO THE LORD, FOR HE HAS TRIUMPHED GLORIOUSLY; THE HORSE AND HIS RIDER HE HAS THROWN INTO THE SEA. THE LORD IS MY STRENGTH AND MY SONG, AND HE HAS BECOME MY SALVATION."

—Exodus 15:1-2

It was finally over. After 400 years in captivity, their adversaries were destroyed before their very eyes. Now, after all those years, they stood on dry ground as their captors were drowned and washed away in the waters of the Red Sea. Israel's deliverance after 400 years of captivity finally came through means of a triumphant flood of water.

The nation of Israel had spent 400 years in captivity under the Egyptians rule. But the Lord heard their prayers, their cries for deliverance, and remembered his promise to their fathers, the promise made to Abraham, to Isaac, and to Jacob.[21] The Lord called and sent Moses, through whom he would deliver his people from the hand of the Egyptians.

The Israelites did not lift a finger to battle their foe. As they stood trapped by the waters of the Red Sea, Moses stretched out his hand over the waters, as the Lord commanded, and it tore in two. Into this divide, Israel walked through the Red Sea on what was now dry ground. They walked out of the land of Egypt and into their freedom.

Once Israel was safe on the other side, Moses again stretched out his hand over the sea, as the Lord commanded. But this time, instead of a miraculous thoroughfare, the waters, which had been divided, barreled back together. The waters of the Red Sea buried the armies of Israel's foes. The Egyptians who once had a seemingly strong grip on the Lord's chosen were no more. With an outstretched hand, their enemies were washed away. As the Red Sea collapsed, their captivity came to an end.

After passively participating in this miraculous deliverance, the nation of Israel burst into song. The shores of the Red Sea were filled with Israel's songs of thanksgiving. The air flooded with the hymnody of all the wonders they had witnessed. The triumphant flood of the Lord had drowned their foes. The Lord was their strength and their song. The Lord was their deliverer.

---

[21] Exodus 2:24.

The psalm writer, in Psalm 106, revisits this account of divine deliverance:

> Yet he saved them for his name's sake, that he might make known his mighty power. He rebuked the Red Sea, and it became dry, and he led them through the deep as through a desert. So he saved them from the hand of the foe and redeemed them from the power of the enemy. And the waters covered their adversaries; not one of them was left (Ps 106:8-11).

Israel, according to the psalmist, was saved because God said he would save them. The Lord rescued Israel because he promised. When God attaches his name and promise to something, it is a done deal.

When our Lord attached his name to us in baptism, promising our rescue from our captors of sin, death, and the power of the devil, it is a done deal. The waters of baptism wash away our sins in a triumphant flood.

Martin Luther connects this story in Exodus with the sacrament of Holy Baptism when he writes in his baptismal prayer, known as the *Flood Prayer*:

> "Who didst drown hardhearted Pharaoh with all his host in the Red Sea and didst lead thy people Israel through the same on dry ground, thereby prefiguring this bath of thy baptism."[22]

---

[22] Martin Luther and Ulrich S. Leupold, *Luther's Works: Liturgy and Hymns*, vol. 53 (Philadelphia, PA: Fortress Press, 1965), 97.

Just as Moses stretched out his hand over the sea, as the Lord commanded, so pastors stretch out their hand with water and the Word, at the Lord's command.[23] Baptism unites us to Christ, our deliverer. Baptismal waters bring us to Christ, the one whose outstretched arms on the cross brought about our salvation and rescue from our captors of sin, death, and the devil.

The Lord is our deliverer. He attaches his powerful name to us in the waters of baptism. Therefore, we too sing of our deliverance. The waters of baptism hydrate our hymnody, our songs of praise. We sing of our salvation, the Lord who delivers us, and has put his holy name upon us in that triumphant flood.

Heavenly Father, you have washed us from our sins in Holy Baptism. You have placed your holy name upon us and made us your own dear children. Send your Holy Spirit to comfort us with the promises you have given us in baptism. Daily repent us, that we may die to sin and live in the forgiveness won for us by your Son's death and resurrection for us. Amen.

> **FOR FURTHER REFLECTION, READ EXODUS 15:1-18.**

---

[23] Matthew 28:18-20.

THE THIRD DAY OF THE SECOND WEEK

Planted in Baptismal Waters

HE IS LIKE A TREE PLANTED BY STREAMS OF WATER THAT YIELDS ITS FRUIT IN ITS SEASON, AND ITS LEAF DOES NOT WITHER. IN ALL THAT HE DOES, HE PROSPERS.

—Psalm 1:3

Plants need water. A tree will anchor its roots deep into the earth just to find the life-giving nourishment a steady supply of water would provide. Without this constant supply of water, the tree would dry up, wither, and perish. Water is essential to life; for plants and for us.

In Psalm one, the psalmist depicts one who is blessed as one who is like "a tree planted by streams of water that yields its fruit in its season, and its leaf does not wither. In all that he does, he prospers" (Ps 1:3). The tree thrives because of the abundant, life-giving, fertile streams of water in which it was planted. It is given life from being planted in the very water that sustains it.

The prophet Jeremiah borrows the psalmist's imagery to describe one who is blessed. He writes,

> Blessed is the man who trusts in the LORD, whose trust is in the LORD. He is like a tree planted by water, that sends out its roots by the stream, and does not fear when heat comes, for its leaves remain green, and is not anxious in the year of drought, for it does not cease to bear fruit (Jer 17:7-8).

On the other hand, the cursed and the wicked are depicted as dehydrated and lifeless. Jeremiah describes those cursed, the one who has not been planted by water, as a shrub in the desert and dwelling in parched, salty places of the wilderness.[24] He goes on to write that the wicked and cursed are such because "they have forsaken the LORD, the fountain of living water" (Jer 17:13).

The psalmist picks up the same imagery of the wicked. They are described as "like chaff that the wind drives away" (Ps 1:4). This chaff, this dried up husk of wheat, is not anchored or planted in water, but is detached from the source of life, empty, and easily taken away by the wind.

---

[24] Jeremiah 17:6.

Through water and God's word, we are planted in streams of baptismal waters. We do not plant ourselves, but we have been planted by our God. Our good and gracious gardener plants us in the rich stream of water flowing from the pierced side of Christ, who hung on the tree of the cross, as we are baptized into his name.[25] The Church Father, Tertullian, describes this connection to baptism when he writes,

> "Never is Christ without water...Onward even to the passion does the witness of baptism last: while He is being surrendered to the cross, water intervenes; witness Pilate's hands: when He is wounded, forth from His side bursts water; witness the soldier's lance!"[26]

This illustration of a tree planted by streams of water is a beautiful image of the baptized life. Once planted, the tree does not leave the water in which it was planted. Rather, the tree dwells in this life-giving stream, bearing its fruit in season.

Christ is at work through water and his word. Through baptism, we are connected to and planted in Christ. His promises to us do not wither. We bear fruit in season because Christ abides with us.

Through the gift of the Holy Spirit, we are those who are blessed. We, who were dried up as chaff and dead in our sins, are given new life as we are baptized into the streams of living water flowing from Jesus' death for us.

---

[25] John 19:34.
[26] Tertullian, *On Baptism* (Savage, MN: Lighthouse Christian Publishing, 2015), 15.

Heavenly Father, you have washed us from our sins in Holy Baptism. You have placed your holy name upon us and made us your own dear children. Send your Holy Spirit to comfort us with the promises you have given us in baptism. Daily repent us, that we may die to sin and live in the forgiveness won for us by your Son's death and resurrection for us. Amen.

> **FOR FURTHER REFLECTION, READ PSALM 1.**

THE FOURTH DAY OF THE SECOND WEEK

Entering God's Kingdom

JESUS ANSWERED, "TRULY, TRULY, I SAY TO YOU, UNLESS ONE IS BORN OF WATER AND THE SPIRIT, HE CANNOT ENTER THE KINGDOM OF GOD. THAT WHICH IS BORN OF THE FLESH IS FLESH, AND THAT WHICH IS BORN OF THE SPIRIT IS SPIRIT."

—John 3:5-6

Throughout the Gospels, Jesus teaches his disciples about the kingdom of God, comparing it to everyday things like seeds, treasure, and feasts.

Jesus compares the kingdom of Heaven to a sower,[27] a mustard seed,[28] a hidden treasure,[29] a net gathering fish,[30]

---

[27] Matthew 13:24.
[28] Luke 13:18-19.
[29] Matthew 13:44.
[30] Matthew 13:47.

and a wedding feast.[31] Matthew, Mark, and Luke record these and many more parables of Jesus, unpacking the mysteries of the kingdom of God.

John does not contain parables in the same way as the synoptic Gospels of Matthew, Mark, and Luke. He does, however, record the words of Jesus as to *how* one enters the kingdom of God. During a meeting at night, Jesus conversed with a curious member of the Sanhedrin (a ruling religious body of the Jews) named Nicodemus.

Jesus tells Nicodemus, "Truly, truly, I say to you, unless one is born again he cannot see the kingdom of God" (John 3:3). Nicodemus was perplexed by Jesus' words. He asked Jesus, how could this be? A second time, Jesus explains, "Truly, truly, I say to you unless one is born of water and the Spirit, he cannot enter the kingdom of God" (John 3:5).

Nicodemus was intrigued by Jesus and his teachings. He confessed, "we know that you are a teacher come from God, for no one can do these signs that you do unless God is with him" (John 3:2). Nicodemus had a private audience with the teacher under the cover of night, but he was left bewildered by Jesus' words that he must be born again. Nicodemus had never come across such a concept before—or so he thought.

---

[31] Matthew 22:2-3.

As Nicodemus repeatedly asked Jesus how this can be, Jesus responds with a rebuke, "Are you the teacher of Israel and yet you do not understand these things?" (John 3:10).

Nicodemus studied and pored over the Scriptures, day after day. He held a position of great religious influence and teaching among the Jews. He familiarized himself with all the laws, the writings of Moses, the Law and the Prophets.

Jesus' words to Nicodemus might have recalled the writings from the prophet Ezekiel. There Lord makes this promise to his people,

> I will sprinkle clean water on you, and you shall be clean from all your uncleannesses, and from all your idols I will cleanse you. And I will give you a new heart, and a new spirit I will put within you (Ezek 36:25-26).

Through parables and conversations like the one with Nicodemus, Jesus reveals the mysteries of the kingdom of God. We are brought into this kingdom as gift, through water and God's word in baptism. As we are sprinkled with the waters of baptism, we are cleansed of our sin and given a new heart.

And yet, as Nicodemus conversed with the very one whom the Law and the Prophets testified of, he remained astounded and unsettled by Jesus' words. He studied the Scriptures to find life—in the keeping of the law. He searched the Scriptures to find the blueprints he must follow to build for himself a secure foundation of righteous living before God.

We must be born again or born from above, Jesus says, of water and the Spirit. In the waters of baptism, our Heavenly Father brings us into his kingdom with new life through water and the word. Through baptism, we are given the gift of the Holy Spirit and wrapped up in Christ's righteousness.

The kingdom of God is like baptism; being born again from water and God's word. In baptism, we are welcomed into the kingdom of God by the Father who loves us, the Son who gave himself for us, and the Holy Spirit who gifts us the faith to believe and confess these gifts.

Heavenly Father, you have washed us from our sins in Holy Baptism. You have placed your holy name upon us and made us your own dear children. Send your Holy Spirit to comfort us with the promises you have given us in baptism. Daily repent us, that we may die to sin and live in the forgiveness won for us by your Son's death and resurrection for us. Amen.

> **FOR FURTHER REFLECTION, READ JOHN 3:1-21.**

Absorbing Our Sin

> THEN JESUS CAME FROM GALILEE TO THE JORDAN TO JOHN, TO BE BAPTIZED BY HIM. JOHN WOULD HAVE PREVENTED HIM, SAYING, "I NEED TO BE BAPTIZED BY YOU, AND DO YOU COME TO ME?" BUT JESUS ANSWERED HIM, "LET IT BE SO NOW, FOR THUS IT IS FITTING FOR US TO FULFILL ALL RIGHTEOUSNESS."
>
> **—Matthew 3:13-15**

On the banks of the Jordan, the last of the Old Testament prophets cried out in the wilderness preparing the way for the Lord. John proclaimed a baptism for the forgiveness of sins. Crowds from Jerusalem, Judea, and all over the region came out to see John the baptizer.

The river seemed to drink up their sins as John baptized in the Jordan river. Confessions flooded the air as the crowds were baptized with a baptism of repentance.

As John was preparing the way, the Lamb of God, the Lord for whom he had been preparing the way, came to him. John the baptizer proclaimed, "Behold, the Lamb of God, who takes away the sin of the world!" (John 1:29). And then, to John's shock, Jesus asked to be baptized.

Jesus was the only one who required no repentance. For one who is without sin, what sins could he confess? The baptizer John, shocked at his request, asked Jesus, "I need to be baptized by you, and do you come to me?" (Matt 3:14). How could the spotless Lamb of God possibly partake in this baptism of repentance?

Jesus told John he must be baptized to fulfill all righteousness. But, what does that mean? The church father Hippolytus explains that in essence, Jesus is telling John,

> "I am the Fulfiller of the law; I seek to leave nothing wanting to its whole fulfillment, that so after me Paul may exclaim, 'Christ is the fulfilling of the law for righteousness to everyone that believeth.'"[32]

Jesus leaves nothing for us to accomplish on our own but does everything for us. He was baptized with a baptism of repentance for us. As Jesus stepped into the waters of the Jordan, he took the place of sinners.[33] Like a sponge, Jesus steps into the Jordan and absorbs our sin.

---

[32] *Ante-Nicene Fathers*, vol. 5, ed. Alexander Roberts, D.D., and James Donaldson, LL.D. (Grand Rapids, MI: WM. B. Eerdmans Publishing Company), 576, Kindle.

[33] 2 Corinthians 5:21.

In Jordan's waters polluted by sin, John baptized Jesus. Jesus, who knew no sin, walked away from his baptism bearing the sins of all people. The river of sin-dirtied water would flow all the way to the cross, where it would be poured out.

In the book of Leviticus, the instructions for the Day of Atonement paint a picture of Jesus' baptism.

> And Aaron shall lay both his hands on the head of the live goat, and confess over it all the iniquities of the people of Israel, and all their transgressions, all their sins. And he shall put them on the head of the goat and send it away into the wilderness by the hand of a man who is in readiness. The goat shall bear all their iniquities on itself to a remote area, and he shall let the goat go free in the wilderness (Lev 16:21-22).

Aaron, the High Priest, was instructed to place his hands on the head of a live goat, transferring the sins of Israel onto the goat. This goat, now carrying the sins of the people, was sent off into the wilderness, taking the sins of the people away. After Jesus was baptized, he was immediately led into the wilderness by the Holy Spirit to be tempted, bearing the iniquities of sinners.[34]

Jesus instructed the disciples to baptize in the name of the Father, and of the Son, and of the Holy Spirit. This baptism is different from John's. This is a baptism of regeneration and renewal of the Holy Spirit. The apostle Paul writes, "he saved us, not because of works done by us in righteousness, but according

---

[34] Matthew 4:1.

to his own mercy, by the washing of regeneration and renewal of the Holy Spirit" (Titus 3:5).

As we are baptized into the name of the Trinity, something happens. A great exchange takes place. Jesus absorbs our sin, and we absorb his righteousness. We are born again, alive by the working of the Holy Spirit.

Jesus placed himself into the waters of the Jordan to be baptized for us. Now, in the waters of our baptism, Jesus again places himself in the waters for us. The Holy Spirit is given to us, not to lead us into the wilderness of temptation, but into the luscious garden of faith where we are connected to Jesus, our life-giving vine.[35] We are loved by our Heavenly Father who has placed his name upon us in baptism. Behold the Lamb of God takes away our sin.

Heavenly Father, you have washed us from our sins in Holy Baptism. You have placed your holy name upon us and made us your own dear children. Send your Holy Spirit to comfort us with the promises you have given us in baptism. Daily repent us, that we may die to sin and live in the forgiveness won for us by your Son's death and resurrection for us. Amen.

> **FOR FURTHER REFLECTION, READ MATTHEW 3:1-17.**

---

[35] John 15:5.

Watery Vestments

> AND THE LORD GOD MADE FOR ADAM AND FOR HIS WIFE GARMENTS OF SKINS AND CLOTHED THEM.
>
> **—Genesis 3:21**

There is a surprising amount of ink spilled on the importance of garments in the Old Testament. Only a few chapters into the book of Genesis, God is springing into action making garments for Adam and Eve. Page ahead in the Old Testament, and you will find chapters detailing the intricacies and requirements for priestly garments.

God is concerned with how his people are clothed, both physically and spiritually. Immediately after the fall into sin in Genesis chapter three, Adam and Eve tried to make garments for themselves. With a little work, they fashioned fig leaf garments. Not the most adequate attire.

As the Lord found Adam and Eve in their sin, shame, and makeshift clothing, he gave them the first promise of Christ who would crush the head of the serpent who had deceived them.[36] The Lord promptly makes Adam and Eve appropriate garments and clothes them, himself. Despite their sin of disobedience to the word of God, despite their abysmal attempts to cover their sins, the Lord freely and mercifully provided.

In the book of Exodus, there is even greater detail demonstrated for the vestments of the priests. The Lord prescribes the pattern and material of the vestments to be made.[37]

The New Testament is filled with the same attention to the importance of garments. From the parable of the wedding feast[38] to the parable of the prodigal son,[39] our Lord is intent on demanding only the best garments. But, what the Lord demands, he also graciously gives. The hymnist Stephen Starke writes,

> "Faith embarked with this discernment: Only God can cover sin, As he took their leafy garments and he clothed their shame with skin."[40]

Adam and Eve's failed attempt to construct their own clothing to cover their sin, led to the first sacrifice or bloodshed recorded

---

[36] Genesis 3:15.
[37] Exodus 28-29.
[38] Matthew 22:1-14.
[39] Luke 15:11-32.
[40] Stephen P. Starke, "Hymn 572," in *Lutheran Service Book: Pew Edition* (Saint Louis, MO: Concordia Publishing House, 1955).

in Scripture. The proper clothing provided by the Lord was that of the skins of an animal. An animal gave its life to clothe Adam and Eve and cover their shame.

Those first garments tailored by God for Adam and Eve were a foreshadowing of watery garments placed upon us in baptism. The apostle Paul writes, "For as many of you as were baptized into Christ have put on Christ" (Gal 3:27).

The Scriptures resonate with the image of Jesus as the Lamb of God, who takes away the sin of the world.[41] The Lamb of God, who takes away our sin, clothes us with himself in the waters of baptism. The theologian, Martin Luther, wrote,

> "Therefore Paul teaches that Baptism is not a sign but the garment of Christ, in fact, that Christ Himself is our garment. Hence Baptism is a very powerful and effective thing."[42]

In the waters of baptism, we are given the garments to enter the wedding feast of the Lamb. We are clothed with Christ and, in turn, receive all the benefits of Christ. We are clothed with his righteousness. God no longer sees the poor attempts we have made to cover our sin. He himself covers us with his own righteousness.

Our Lord is intent that we are clothed with the best. In the waters of baptism, he himself clothes us. We are well-dressed

---

[41] John 1:29.

[42] Martin Luther, *Luther's Works: Lectures on Galatians 1535, Chapters 1-4*, vol. 26, ed. Jaroslav Pelikan (Saint Louis, MO: Concordia Publishing House, 1963), 353.

in the garments of our great High Priest who shed his blood for us that we may be covered and welcomed into the joyous wedding feast that has no end.

Heavenly Father, you have washed us from our sins in Holy Baptism. You have placed your holy name upon us and made us your own dear children. Send your Holy Spirit to comfort us with the promises you have given us in baptism. Daily repent us, that we may die to sin and live in the forgiveness won for us by your Son's death and resurrection for us. Amen.

> **FOR FURTHER REFLECTION, READ GENESIS 3:1-24.**

An Extravagant Father

BUT THE FATHER SAID TO HIS SERVANTS, "BRING QUICKLY THE BEST ROBE, AND PUT IT ON HIM, AND PUT A RING ON HIS HAND, AND SHOES ON HIS FEET. AND BRING THE FATTENED CALF AND KILL IT, AND LET US EAT AND CELEBRATE.'

—Luke 15:22-23

As the father's youngest son was feeding the pigs, he finally came to his senses, or so he thought. Maybe, just maybe, with the right apology and speech, his father would take him back. Though, not as a son, of course. He knew that possibility was long gone.

Anything was better than life in the far country. He had demanded his inheritance, took his father's money and wasted it. He left his family and started a new life for himself in the far country. After spending everything, he became desperate. He had found a job feeding pigs, which were unclean animals. He had hit rock bottom. The pigs' food had even become appetizing.

Any chance that his father might take him on as a hired servant was a better choice than staying in the far country. So, after rehearsing an apologetic speech, the son set out toward home. He was returning hungry and disgraced.

While the son was still a long way off, his father ran and lovingly embraced his son. It was almost as if the father was ignorant of the sins of his prodigal son.

The son knew that now was his chance. In the middle of his father's embrace, he started into his apologetic speech. If his repentance was sincere enough, and his father heard him out, maybe he could become one of his father's hired servants.

> "Father, I have sinned against heaven and before you. I am no longer worthy to be called your son." But the father said to his servants, "Bring quickly the best robe, and put it on him, and put a ring on his hand, and shoes on his feet. And bring the fattened calf and kill it, and let us eat and celebrate. For this my son was dead, and is alive again; he was lost, and is found." And they began to celebrate (Luke 15:21-24).

The son never finished his speech. His father interrupted him. It's almost as if his father didn't even hear his son's polished apology. He didn't even acknowledge his son's speech. The father was too busy calling out in a hurry to his servants to bring the best of the best for his son. The father even called for the fattened calf to be killed so that they could have a celebratory feast. Nothing the son did in the far country, nor his speech, seemed to matter. Despite the actions of the prodigal son, the attitude and actions of the father were far more extravagant.

The son's repentance was all wrong. He did not understand the graciousness of his father. Before his father so rudely interrupted him, he was about to ask for a contract. He wanted his father to take him on as one who is paid a wage for his work.

The father refused to give his son the opportunity to ask for a contract. The father was always his father, regardless of how his son acted. He does not deal with his lost child in the way of the law. The father spares no expense to celebrate the return of his lost child. The son's return was not marked by a long journey home, but by his father running to him while he was still a long way off.

Our Heavenly Father will have nothing of our faulty repentance. While we were still a long way off, our Heavenly Father came running towards us. The apostle Paul writes, "but God shows his love for us in that while we were still sinners, Christ died for us" (Rom 5:8).

While we were still sinners, our Heavenly Father embraced us in the waters of baptism, welcoming us home as his beloved children. Our Heavenly Father wastes no time dressing us with the finest robe in baptism, the robe of Christ.[43] Jesus, the fattened calf, was crucified for us that we might eat and celebrate at the wedding feast of the Lamb.

The past is forgotten. The Lord says, "I, I am he who blots out your transgressions for my own sake, and I will not remember your sins" (Isa 43:25). Our sins are washed away in the waters of baptism. Through water and the Word, we become recipients of all the gifts our Heavenly Father graciously gives us. We were dead in our trespasses and sins but are alive again by water and the Word. And now that the Triune God has brought us home and done everything for us, we celebrate!

Heavenly Father, you have washed us from our sins in Holy Baptism. You have placed your holy name upon us and made us your own dear children. Send your Holy Spirit to comfort us with the promises you have given us in baptism. Daily repent us, that we may die to sin and live in the forgiveness won for us by your Son's death and resurrection for us. Amen.

> **FOR FURTHER REFLECTION, READ LUKE 15:1-32.**

---

[43] Galatians 3:27.

Water and the Word

JESUS SAID TO THE SERVANTS, "FILL THE JARS WITH WATER." AND THEY FILLED THEM UP TO THE BRIM. AND HE SAID TO THEM, "NOW DRAW SOME OUT AND TAKE IT TO THE MASTER OF THE FEAST." SO THEY TOOK IT. WHEN THE MASTER OF THE FEAST TASTED THE WATER NOW BECOME WINE, AND DID NOT KNOW WHERE IT CAME FROM (THOUGH THE SERVANTS WHO HAD DRAWN THE WATER KNEW), THE MASTER OF THE FEAST CALLED THE BRIDEGROOM.

—John 2:7-9

The party was about to come to an abrupt end. Jesus' mother approached him with four short celebration-ending words, "They have no wine" (John 2:3). Without wine, there is no wedding feast. Without wine, there is nothing to drink. Without wine, the party is dead.

It was on the third day, writes the apostle John, that the wedding feast at Cana was about to come to a screeching halt. It was on the third day in which Jesus' mother looked to him to resurrect what would soon be a dead party.

Although Jesus gently told his mother, "My hour has not yet come" (John 2:4), he seemingly couldn't help but make sure the party continued. Jesus instructed the servants at the wedding to fill the purification jars with water and then take some of it to the master of the feast.

> When the master of the feast tasted the water now become wine...the master of the feast called the bridegroom and said to him, "Everyone serves the good wine first, and when people have drunk freely, then the poor wine. But you have kept the good wine until now" (John 2:9-10).

On the third day, at a wedding celebration which was as good as dead in Cana, Jesus took water combined with his word and brought the celebration back to life—*abundantly*. Without his word and command, the party would have ended.

On the third day, Jesus resurrected the wedding feast. The water turned to wine with Jesus' word was even better than the top-shelf wine they began with at the celebration. The wine created from water and Jesus' word was the best of the best.

The servants had a front-row seat to watch in awe as Jesus, Word of God made flesh, turned water into wine. They had no power in themselves. No decision to draw water could have transformed it into wine. Jesus' words and command did it all. Jesus was and is the actor and the giver.

Throughout the Gospels, Jesus speaks in parables of the kingdom of heaven to a grand wedding feast celebration: a joyful gathering between his beloved bride (the church) and himself (the bridegroom).[44] Through water and the word, we are brought into this wedding feast of the Lamb.[45]

To be baptized is to be brought into the party. Just as Jesus was the actor and giver in Cana, so too is he the actor and giver in the gift of baptism. Jesus freely gives and we graciously receive. The reformer, Martin Luther, writes,

> "Baptism is simply water and God's Word in and with each other; that is, when the Word accompanies the water, Baptism is valid, even though faith be lacking. For my faith does not constitute Baptism but receives it."[46]

Our faith does not make baptism. Faith receives the gift of the forgiveness of our sins and gift of the Holy Spirit through baptism. Through water and the Word, Jesus pours out only the best gifts to us.

Our Lord gives abundantly. Through water connected to God's word, we receive a promise; our sins are forgiven, we are clothed

---

[44] Matthew 25:1-13; Luke 14:12-24.
[45] Revelation 19:9.
[46] LC IV 53.

with Christ, we will be raised in a resurrection like his,[47] and we will be welcomed into the wedding feast of the Lamb to celebrate with all the saints.

Jesus provided the wine for a wedding celebration with his word and some jugs of water. With his Word and ordinary water, Jesus has provided everything necessary for our salvation. Our sinful nature is buried with Christ in baptism, and we are clothed with only the best, Christ's righteousness.[48] We are given the gift of the Holy Spirit and made children of our Heavenly Father.

Heavenly Father, you have washed us from our sins in Holy Baptism. You have placed your holy name upon us and made us your own dear children. Send your Holy Spirit to comfort us with the promises you have given us in baptism. Daily repent us, that we may die to sin and live in the forgiveness won for us by your Son's death and resurrection for us. Amen.

> **FOR FURTHER REFLECTION, READ JOHN 2:1-12.**

---

[47] Romans 6:5.
[48] Galatians 3:27.

WEEK THREE

A Baptismal Exorcism

AND YOU WERE DEAD IN THE TRESPASSES AND SINS IN WHICH YOU ONCE WALKED, FOLLOWING THE COURSE OF THIS WORLD, FOLLOWING THE PRINCE OF THE POWER OF THE AIR, THE SPIRIT THAT IS NOW AT WORK IN THE SONS OF DISOBEDIENCE—AMONG WHOM WE ALL ONCE LIVED

—Ephesians 2:1-3

In the book of Ephesians, the apostle Paul speaks with deep gravity about our state before baptism, before we have been united to Christ. He writes that we were dead in our trespasses. In fact, it gets even worse. We were not only dead to God because of our sin; we were slaves, carrying out the will of the prince of the power of the air, Satan.

Those who are dead cannot raise themselves. Children of wrath, as Paul describes our life outside of Christ, cannot make themselves children of God. The apostle's description of our sinful nature is not only that which is passively dead in transgressions, but actively fighting against God.

We made ourselves enemies of God through our sin, actively rebelling against his word. But God being rich in mercy did not forsake us and leave us in captivity of our sin. In sharp contrast to our actions and trespasses which brought death, the apostle expounds on what God has accomplished for us in Christ. Paul writes, "But God, being rich in mercy, because of the great love with which he loved us, even when we were dead in our trespasses, made us alive together with Christ" (Eph 2:4-5).

The theologian, Dr. Norman Nagel, speaks about God's work of freeing us from the domain of Satan through baptism. He writes,

> By Baptism the Lord saves and makes us his own. The only alternative to belonging to him is belonging to the devil. Hence Satan must be banished and renounced...The dominion of Satan is the dominion of sin. Baptism frees us from this.[49]

Our Lord snatches us from the kingdom of Satan, the prince of the power of the air. We no longer belong to the devil. We have the name of the triune God placed upon us in baptism, and we

---

[49] Norman E. Nagel, "Holy Baptism," in *Lutheran Worship: History and Practice*, ed. Fred L. Precht (Saint Louis: Concordia Publishing House, 1993), 273.

are brought into the kingdom of God. Our risen Lord paid the debt of death for our transgressions. God, being rich in mercy, baptized us, freeing us from the power that sin, death, and the devil once had over us.

In his work, *The Order of Baptism* (1523), the reformer, Martin Luther, wrote a liturgy (or worship service) of baptism in a somewhat strange manner. He instructs the service of baptism begin with these words, "Depart thou unclean spirit and give room to the Holy Spirit."[50]

Luther saw the work of God in baptism as comparable to an exorcism. In Holy Baptism, God alone acts. Just as Jesus drove out demons through his word, our rescue comes through Jesus' almighty word. We cannot make ourselves children of God. We cannot cleanse ourselves of our sin. Life and rescue must come from the outside.

Baptism emboldens us to proclaim our merciful Lord who calls us his own and renounce the devil and our sinful nature. We are baptized and set free! We are free to confess and proclaim the gracious God who saved us from the domain of sin, death, and the devil, through water and his word.

With confidence, we can sing with the hymnist, Erdmann Neumeister,

---

[50] Martin Luther, *Luther's Works, Volume 53: Liturgy and Hymns*, ed. Ulrich S. Leupold, gen. ed. Helmut T. Lehmann (Philadelphia: Fortress Press, 1965), 96.

> "Satan, hear this proclamation: I am baptized into Christ!... Now that to the font I've traveled, All your might has come unraveled, And, against your tyranny, God, my Lord, unites with me!"[51]

We, who were once enemies of God, are now children of God through baptism. Our Lord promises his baptized saints that he will never leave us.[52] We have been marked and named in Holy Baptism as his own. Nothing can separate us from the promise our Lord has made to us in our baptism.[53] Our sins are forgiven. Satan, with all his power over us, has been driven out by our Redeemer. We are his baptized, beloved saints.

Heavenly Father, you have joined us to your Son in Holy Baptism. Through ordinary water connected to your almighty and gracious Word, you have gifted us with your Holy Spirit. Remember all your promises to us as we live as your baptized children, forgiven and sanctified through the work of your Son. Graciously bring us to daily repentance and forgive our sins according to your promise. Amen.

FOR FURTHER REFLECTION, READ EPHESIANS 2:1-22.

---

[51] Erdmann Neumeister, "Hymn 594," in *Lutheran Service Book: Pew Edition* (Saint Louis, MO: Concordia Publishing House, 2006).

[52] Matthew 28:20.

[53] Romans 8:38-39.

THE SECOND DAY OF THE THIRD WEEK

Ordinary Water

SO HE WENT DOWN AND DIPPED HIMSELF SEVEN TIMES IN THE JORDAN, ACCORDING TO THE WORD OF THE MAN OF GOD, AND HIS FLESH WAS RESTORED LIKE THE FLESH OF A LITTLE CHILD, AND HE WAS CLEAN.

—2 Kings 5:14

Naaman was a decorated commander for one of the most powerful armies in Syria. He was a courageous leader. But he also had leprosy. And no number of military victories or valor could remove his sickness. Naaman could not heal himself.

Upon learning about a prophet in Israel, Naaman finds renewed hope. Maybe, just maybe, he could finally be free of the leprosy that plagued him. After speaking with his king, Naaman sets off to meet with the king of Israel. Understanding the significance of first impressions, Naaman's king sent him to Israel with a generous bounty of gifts for the king of Israel.

However, instead of receiving this diplomatic gift, the king of Israel becomes overwhelmed with sorrow to the point of tearing his clothes. Naaman cannot buy or bribe his way into being healed. The king of Israel knows he is powerless to heal Naaman of his leprosy.

When the prophet Elisha hears of Naaman's visit, he intervenes, requesting Naaman come to his house. There was just one problem. As a result of Naaman's leprosy, he was unclean according to Levitical law.

To avoid the risk of himself becoming unclean, Elisha sent a messenger out to Naaman instead of meeting with him in person. The message from the prophet was this, "Go and wash in the Jordan seven times, and your flesh shall be restored, and you shall be clean" (2 Kgs 5:10).

Naaman was outraged, insulted. He expected more from this great prophet in Israel. He at least expected the prophet to come out to him. Ultimately, he wanted a magic show from Elisha. He wanted Elisha to wave his hand over his leprosy and call on the name of the Lord his God and cure him.

Didn't the prophet know this wasn't even the best river? There was nothing special about the prophet's instructions. But, at the encouragement of his servants, Naaman begrudgingly went to the Jordan River. Naaman went and dipped himself seven times in the Jordan as Elisha instructed and he was healed, according to the prophet's word. In fact, he was healed so much that his flesh was not only restored but restored to that "like the flesh of a little child" (2 Kgs 5:14).

The Jordan River, where Naaman's leprosy was taken away, is the same river where Jesus was later baptized. It was on the banks of the river that John declared, "Behold, the Lamb of God, who takes away the sin of the world" (John 1:29). It was at the Jordan River that Jesus was baptized and anointed with our spiritual leprosy, our sin.

The reverse happens in Jesus' baptism. He goes in spotless and sinless and comes out bearing our dirt, our disease of sin. Through water and his Word, we pick up his righteousness in the waters of baptism and are made clean. As spiritual lepers, we too were unable to heal ourselves. We needed someone outside of us to make us clean and take away our sin.

Baptism, much like Naaman's washing in the Jordan River, is not an outwardly extravagant event. However, something extraordinary unfolds in the ordinary waters of baptism. God does the extravagant: he cleanses us of our sin, marks us with the name of the Trinity, and makes us children of our Heavenly Father. With a few splashes of water, Jesus soaks up our sin, and we are drenched with his righteousness.

Unlike Naaman, we do not have to make a journey to a specific body of water to be made clean. The efficacy of Holy Baptism doesn't reside in the water itself, or even in the baptized. Any water used to baptize in union with God's word washes away sins. In his baptismal prayer, Martin Luther describes the ordinary waters of baptism in this way,

> "Through the baptism of thy dear Child, our Lord Jesus Christ, hast consecrated and set apart the Jordan and all water as a salutary flood and a rich and full washing away of sins."[54]

The saving work of baptism is in the Word attached to the waters of baptism. There, Jesus restores us, there we are given his righteousness and life. In the flood of baptism, our sinful nature is drowned, and a new person rises in Christ. For us, Jesus was baptized, so that in our baptism, he would make us clean.

Heavenly Father, you have joined us to your Son in Holy Baptism. Through ordinary water connected to your almighty and gracious Word, you have gifted us with your Holy Spirit. Remember all your promises to us as we live as your baptized children, forgiven and sanctified through the work of your Son. Graciously bring us to daily repentance and forgive our sins according to your promise. Amen.

> **FOR FURTHER REFLECTION, READ 2 KINGS 5:1-14.**

---

[54] Martin Luther, *Luther's Works: Liturgy and Hymns*, vol. 53, ed. Ulrich S. Leupold (Philadelphia, PA: Fortress Press, 1965), 107.

Baptismal Hyssop

PURGE ME WITH HYSSOP, AND I SHALL BE CLEAN; WASH ME, AND I SHALL BE WHITER THAN SNOW.

—*Psalm 51:7*

In the Old Testament book of Leviticus, God gave his people a set of laws regarding cleanliness. According to Levitical law, anything unclean transferred its impurity to those who touched it. However, when Jesus touches what is impure or unclean, the reverse happens.

In the book of Numbers, the purification laws detail the procedure for cleansing upon contact with a dead body. The purification protocol involves using the hyssop plant to sprinkle water on anything that is unclean on the third and seventh day. On the evening of the seventh day, after the unclean has washed, they will be clean. They then enter the eighth day fully purified.[55]

---

[55] Numbers 19:18-19.

As for those unclean because of a skin condition such as leprosy, the book of Leviticus provides instruction for restoration as well. If someone is healed of their leprosy, they must undergo a seven-day purification protocol as well, ahead of their complete restoration on the eighth day. This procedure also involves the hyssop plant. The priest is to dip the hyssop plant in blood and water, then sprinkle the individual who has been cured of leprosy.[56]

As Jesus travels preaching and teaching about the kingdom of heaven, he heals all kinds of diseases. He makes the unclean, clean. He has mercy on those who cry out to him as the leper in Mark's Gospel,

> And a leper came to him, imploring him, and kneeling said to him, 'If you will, you can make me clean.' Moved with pity, [Jesus] stretched out his hand and touched him and said to him, 'I will; be clean.' And immediately the leprosy left him, and he was made clean (Mark 1:40-42).

In Psalm 51, the psalmist David cries out in a similar way for the Lord to have mercy on him and make him clean. David writes,

> Have mercy on me, O God, according to your steadfast love; according to your abundant mercy blot out my transgressions. Wash me thoroughly from my iniquity, and cleanse me from my sin!... Purge me with hyssop, and I shall be clean; wash me, and I shall be whiter than snow (Ps 51:1-2, 7).

---

[56] Leviticus 14:6-7.

Moved with pity, Jesus stretched out his hands on the cross. As he stretched out his nail pierced hands, Jesus says to us, "I will; be clean." Jesus took our impurity upon himself and makes us clean with his righteousness.

In this way Jesus is our cleansing hyssop. In the waters of baptism, we are sprinkled with the water and the word as Jesus, our baptismal hyssop, cleanses us of all unrighteousness.

In the book of Exodus, we encounter another instruction from the Lord regarding the use of the hyssop plant. Each household was to mark their doorposts with the blood of the Passover lamb using hyssop, and the Lord spared the life of the firstborn in those houses marked with the blood of the lamb.[57] In baptism, the water and the Word mark us with the saving blood of Christ, our Paschal Lamb.

Jesus tells us that the Scriptures point to himself and his redemptive work for us.[58] All these Levitical laws find their fulfillment in Christ.

It is Jesus who purifies us. He washes us in the flood of baptism and makes us whiter than snow with his purity, his righteousness. Jesus wills that we be cleansed from our sin and live forever with him in righteousness. According to his steadfast love and abundant mercy, in baptism, our transgressions are

---
[57] Exodus 12:22.
[58] John 5:39.

forever blotted out in the death of the Lamb of God. In Christ, our consciences are forever cleansed, and we arise from the deadness of sin to new life in him.

Heavenly Father, you have joined us to your Son in Holy Baptism. Through ordinary water connected to your almighty and gracious Word, you have gifted us with your Holy Spirit. Remember all your promises to us as we live as your baptized children, forgiven and sanctified through the work of your Son. Graciously bring us to daily repentance and forgive our sins according to your promise.

Amen.

> **FOR FURTHER REFLECTION, READ PSALM 51.**

Washing of Regeneration

HE SAVED US, NOT BECAUSE OF WORKS DONE BY US IN RIGHTEOUSNESS, BUT ACCORDING TO HIS OWN MERCY, BY THE WASHING OF REGENERATION AND RENEWAL OF THE HOLY SPIRIT.

—Titus 3:5

Reading the apostle Paul's letters or epistles to the churches throughout the Mediterranean feels a little like looking into someone else's mail. Throughout his epistles in the New Testament, Paul addresses specific circumstances within the church. He admonishes and commends the churches and saints within them.

In his letter to Titus, Paul writes to his companion in the ministry. In his greeting, Paul writes, "To Titus, my true child in a common faith: Grace and peace from God the Father and Christ Jesus our Savior" (Titus 1:4). He exhorts

Titus to continue in the teaching of sound doctrine and encourages good works in light of the gospel.

As Paul encourages Titus towards good works in his vocation, he interrupts his letter to bring Titus back to what God did in baptism. Paul writes,

> But when the goodness and loving kindness of God our Savior appeared, he saved us, not because of works done by us in righteousness, but according to his own mercy, by the washing of regeneration and renewal of the Holy Spirit, whom he poured out on us richly through Jesus Christ our Savior, so that being justified by his grace we might become heirs according to the hope of eternal life (Titus 3:4-7).

In the middle of Paul's exhortation to show love and care for our neighbor, he makes it clear that works we do are of no use for our salvation. We can do nothing to earn or merit our salvation. Everything, including baptism, is a pure and gracious gift.

Baptism is not a simple ritual we carry out to prove our faith or commitment to God. Baptism is abundantly more! This miraculous bath of regeneration and renewal of the Holy Spirit saves us, who are dead in our trespasses, *because* it is not dependent on us.

Paul writes in the book of Romans that no one seeks after God. We have no good works to offer and no understanding.[59]

---

[59] Romans 3:10-12.

We were completely and devastatingly dead in our sins.[60] But because of the loving kindness of our Savior and his works, through the washing of regeneration of the Holy Spirit, we are welcomed home as children of our Heavenly Father.

The reformer, Martin Luther, puts it this way,

> "Note well, therefore, that baptism is water with the Word of God, not water and my faith. My faith does not make the baptism but rather receives the baptism, no matter whether the person being baptized believes or not; for baptism is not dependent upon my faith but upon God's Word."[61]

Baptism is not a promise we make to God, but a gift and a promise made to us by the Father, Son, and Holy Spirit. It is a promise of sins forgiven and life everlasting. It is a promise that though we sin daily, the Lord repents us, bringing us back to our baptism, back to where he has promised to be for us with the forgiveness of sins and grace.

As Paul wraps up his letter to Titus, he again exhorts his dear friend in the ministry toward good works. He encourages the baptized to devote themselves to good works within their vocation. In light of all God has gifted us through the water and the Word, we are free to love, serve, and forgive those around us,

---

[60] Ephesians 2:4-5.
[61] Martin Luther, *Luther's Works, Volume 51: Sermons 1*, ed. and trans. John W. Doberstein, gen. ed. Helmut T. Lehmann (Philadelphia: Muhlenberg Press, 1959), 186.

just as we have been loved, served, and forgiven by the Father, Son, and Holy Spirit in baptism.

Heavenly Father, you have joined us to your Son in Holy Baptism. Through ordinary water connected to your almighty and gracious Word, you have gifted us with your Holy Spirit. Remember all your promises to us as we live as your baptized children, forgiven and sanctified through the work of your Son. Graciously bring us to daily repentance and forgive our sins according to your promise.
Amen.

> **FOR FURTHER REFLECTION, READ TITUS 3:1-15.**

THE FIFTH DAY OF THE THIRD WEEK

Caught in the Word

"DO NOT BE AFRAID; FROM NOW ON YOU WILL BE CATCHING MEN."

—Luke 5:10

After an exhausting night of fishing with nothing to show for their efforts, the weary fishermen were cleaning up and preparing to go home. But just as they were washing their nets, Jesus arrived. Sitting in Simon's boat, Jesus began to teach the crowd by the lake. After Jesus had finished teaching the crowd, he turned to Simon and said, "Put out into the deep and let down your nets for a catch" (Luke 5:4). Simon was reluctant. After working all night without success, it was becoming more unlikely as the day went on that he would be able to draw in a catch of fish. "But," Simon said, "at your word I will let down the nets" (Luke 5:5).

As they let down their nets according to the Word, something happened. Their nets tugged sharply, weighed down by an unexpected, thrashing haul of fish. Overwhelmed, they immediately started calling for help from their partners. There were too many fish to count as their boats started glistening with the scaly, thrashing, fish. Not only did their nets begin to break from the weight of it all, but their boats also began taking on water as the weight of the fish overwhelmed their vessels.

As Simon (who is also called Peter) witnessed what had just happened, he fell before Jesus confessing his sin. Overwhelmed by the miraculous catch, Peter fell at Jesus' feet, confessing his unworthiness. "Depart from me, for I am a sinful man, O Lord" (Luke 5:8). But, Jesus had mercy on Peter and gently spoke to the fear filled fisherman, "Do not be afraid from now on you will be catching men" (Luke 5:10).

Jesus tells Peter that from now on, he will be a different kind of fisherman. And, simply at the word of Jesus, Peter left everything and followed him.

Just as these multitudes of fish were caught up in the fishermen's nets by the word of God, so too we are caught up in the word of God in our baptism. We are drawn out of the murky depths of our sin and death and placed into the saving waters of Holy Baptism. It is there, in the waters of baptism, in the forgiveness of sins and the promise of life everlasting, that we continue to dwell.

The early church father, Tertullian, writes of baptism,

"But we, little fishes, after the example of our ΙΧΘΥΣ Jesus Christ, are born in water, nor have we safety in any other way than by permanently abiding in water; so that most monstrous creature, who had no right to teach even sound doctrine, knew full well how to kill the little fishes, by taking them away from the water!"[62]

We don't say "I was baptized" as if it's a past event. We say, "I am baptized!" because it's a present reality that defines who we are today. We are little fish dwelling in the baptismal waters of life. We have been watered and worded at the baptismal font and brought into the church through the net of the gospel. Jesus said, "And I, when I am lifted up from the earth, will draw all people to myself" (John 12:32). In his death for our sins, Jesus casts the net and draws us into his death and resurrection for us.

Just as the fishermen were overwhelmed by the abundance of fish so much so that their nets began to break and their boats began to sink, so too we are weighed down by the gifts delivered to us in our baptism. We have received grace upon grace, as John writes in his Gospel.[63]

In our baptism, we forever swim and live in the bottomless ocean of forgiveness. Not by our own strength, but by the word of the Lord, we have been pulled into the forgiveness of sins and abundant life as we are baptized in the name of the Father, Son, and Holy Spirit. To remember our baptism is to

---

[62] Tertullian, *On Baptism* (Savage, MN: Lighthouse Christian Publishing, 2015), 6.
[63] John 1:16.

turn in repentance to our Lord, confessing our sin with Peter and Isaiah, only to hear the gentle, comforting voice of Jesus say, "Do not be afraid, your sins are forgiven."

Heavenly Father, you have joined us to your Son in Holy Baptism. Through ordinary water connected to your almighty and gracious Word, you have gifted us with your Holy Spirit. Remember all your promises to us as we live as your baptized children, forgiven and sanctified through the work of your Son. Graciously bring us to daily repentance and forgive our sins according to your promise. Amen.

FOR FURTHER REFLECTION, READ LUKE 5:1-11.

THE SIXTH DAY OF THE THIRD WEEK

Faithed

GO, THEREFORE AND MAKE DISCIPLES OF ALL NATIONS, BAPTIZING THEM IN THE NAME OF THE FATHER AND OF THE SON AND OF THE HOLY SPIRIT, TEACHING THEM TO OBSERVE ALL THAT I HAVE COMMANDED YOU. AND BEHOLD, I AM WITH YOU ALWAYS, TO THE END OF THE AGE.

—Matthew 28:19-20

After all of the miracles they had seen, some still doubted. They witnessed Jesus heal the sick and even raise the dead. And yet, still their faith wavered. Jesus called them each by name to follow him but still they faltered. They had seen their Lord crucified, dead, buried, and alive again on the third day. But still, they could not by their own strength believe.

Matthew recounts in his Gospel that when the disciples gathered on a mountain in Galilee, as Jesus had instructed them, "when they saw him they worshiped him, but some doubted" (Matt 28:17).

In the midst of his own disciples' unbelief, Jesus gives them the solution: the gift of baptism. He instructed them on the mountain to go and make disciples, baptizing in the name of the Father and of the Son and of the Holy Spirit.

The efficacy of baptism does not rest in the individual being baptized, nor does it come from the water itself. The power of baptism resides in the word of God, the promises of Jesus, and the Holy Spirit given in this sacramental gift. Jesus said to his disciples, "All authority in heaven and on earth has been given to me" (Matt 28:18). Jesus, who died and rose again for us, has the authority to deliver what he promises.

A miracle takes place as unbelief and doubt is cast out by the working of the Holy Spirit. The Word grabs hold of us in baptism and binds himself to us. Through water and the Word, we are faithed back to life, given confidence to believe the promises of God. The theologian, Gerhard Forde, writes of the sacrament of Holy Baptism,

> "It is a Word of God addressed directly and concretely to us. It has our name on it. There is no mistake about to whom it may be addressed.... It is concretely and unmistakably 'for you.' God claims you and you are sealed with the sign of the cross forever."[64]

When faced with doubt and unbelief, we cling to the certainty of God's work for us in baptism. Our faith doesn't depend on

---

[64] Gerhard O. Forde, *Theology is for Proclamation* (Minneapolis: Fortress Press, 1990), 166.

our feelings; it rests solely on our Lord's unshakable promise to us. The comfort we have in baptism is that our Lord speaks directly and concretely to us, declaring, "Fear not, for I have redeemed you; I have called you by name, you are mine" (Isa 43:1). The Holy Spirit creates the faith we cannot produce ourselves as the Father, Son, and Holy Spirit water and word us back to life.

The gospel is directly applied specifically to us in baptism. Jesus spoke words of peace to his doubting disciple, Thomas, "Peace be with you...Put your finger here, and see my hands; and put out your hand and place it in my side. Do not disbelieve, but believe" (John 20:26-27). The same Jesus who called his unbelieving disciple to faith is there with us in our baptism giving us the gift of the Holy Spirit, the gift of faith.

After instituting this sacrament of Holy Baptism, Jesus comforts us with the promise, "And behold, I am with you always, to the end of the age" (Matt 28:20). Jesus will never forsake those upon whom he places his name. He promises to be with us to the end of the age delivering his good gospel gifts of the forgiveness of sins, life, and salvation.

Heavenly Father, you have joined us to your Son in Holy Baptism. Through ordinary water connected to your almighty and gracious Word, you have gifted us with your Holy Spirit. Remember all your promises to us as we live as your baptized children, forgiven and sanctified through the work of your Son. Graciously bring us to daily repentance and forgive our sins according to your promise. Amen.

> **FOR FURTHER REFLECTION, READ ROMANS 8:1-17.**

THE SEVENTH DAY OF THE THIRD WEEK

Entombed in the Water

DO YOU NOT KNOW THAT ALL OF US WHO HAVE BEEN BAPTIZED INTO CHRIST JESUS WERE BAPTIZED INTO HIS DEATH? WE WERE BURIED THEREFORE WITH HIM BY BAPTISM INTO DEATH, IN ORDER THAT, JUST AS CHRIST WAS RAISED FROM THE DEAD BY THE GLORY OF THE FATHER, WE TOO MIGHT WALK IN NEWNESS OF LIFE.

—Romans 6:3-4

Within the pages of Romans, the apostle Paul has written a guide for living the baptized life. The apostle delves into the depths of the mysteries of what our God has done for us in these life-giving waters.

For Paul, the gospel is, as he writes in the first chapter, "the power of God for salvation to everyone who believes" (Rom 1:16). The apostle makes clear from the beginning that we are justified apart from our own works. It is the gospel, the power of God and not our own strength, which works salvation. We have been gifted Christ's righteousness. With each chapter, the book of Romans reverberates more and more with the enormity of the gospel.

As the pages overflow with God's immense grace, Paul seemingly takes a step back as chapter six begins. The apostle asks, "What shall we say then? Are we to continue in sin that grace may abound?" (Rom 6:1). Instead of countering his own question with the law, Paul doubles down on the gospel by exhorting the Romans to remember their baptism.

Encased in chapter six of Romans is a beautiful portrait of the reality Holy Baptism bestows on the baptized. The baptized life is a life hidden in Christ. Baptism is the gospel, the power of God for salvation.

The God who created all things through his almighty Word, made his holy Son, who knew no sin, to become our sin.[65] As Jesus laid down his life in death for us and was buried, our sins went fully with him into his tomb. He who made his Son to be our sin, now makes us, through baptism, the righteousness of his holy Son.

In baptism, we are united with Christ in his death and buried with him. In the baptismal font, our sins are buried in the tomb

---

[65] 2 Corinthians 5:21.

and our sinful nature is drowned in the grave. The theologian, Dr. Robert Kolb, describes this baptismal burial when he states, "He buries sinners in Christ's tomb, the only place in his universe where he no longer looks."[66]

Once, for all, in his death, Christ has buried our sin with himself. All our sins, past, present, and future, have been crucified and buried with Christ.

Through Holy Baptism, the triune God grabs hold of us by water and the Word and unites us with Christ our Lord in his death, burial, *and* resurrection. The apostle writes, "For if we have been united with him in a death like his, we shall certainly be united with him in a resurrection like his" (Rom 6:5).

Baptism is not merely a simple ritual carried out by the church. Baptism is the power of God for salvation. Baptism is the gospel. Baptism is Jesus given through water and the word of God.

As baptized children of God, we are free from our sins and alive in Christ, our Lord. Paul continues in the book of Romans to write of the daily struggle of the sinful nature fighting against this new life in Christ. We remain simultaneously sinners and saints. Our sinful nature fights and tries to swim against the waves of baptism but in the end will not prevail.

---

[66] Robert Kolb, *The Christian Faith: A Lutheran Exposition* (Saint Louis, MO: Concordia Publishing House, 1993), 216.

Our sin does not have the final word. The final word belongs to our God who has that final word as he baptizes us, declaring us as his own. He places us into the care and person of Christ through baptism. Our sins are buried in that watery grave, and we are free to live in the life of Christ—the life of love and service to our neighbors gifted to us.

Heavenly Father, you have joined us to your Son in Holy Baptism. Through ordinary water connected to your almighty and gracious Word, you have gifted us with your Holy Spirit. Remember all your promises to us as we live as your baptized children, forgiven and sanctified through the work of your Son. Graciously bring us to daily repentance and forgive our sins according to your promise. Amen.

> **FOR FURTHER REFLECTION, READ ROMANS 6:1-14.**

THE EIGHTH DAY OF THE THIRD WEEK

A New Identity

IN HIM ALSO YOU WERE CIRCUMCISED WITH A CIRCUMCISION MADE WITHOUT HANDS, BY PUTTING OFF THE BODY OF THE FLESH, BY THE CIRCUMCISION OF CHRIST, HAVING BEEN BURIED WITH HIM IN BAPTISM, IN WHICH YOU WERE ALSO RAISED WITH HIM THROUGH FAITH IN THE POWERFUL WORKING OF GOD, WHO RAISED HIM FROM THE DEAD.

—Colossians 2:11-12

In the deep velvety darkness, an array of uncountable stars pierced the night sky. The word of the Lord came to Abraham and said, "Look toward heaven, and number the stars, if you are able to number them… So shall your offspring be" (Gen 15:5). The stars became a sign of the promise. As the Lord flooded Abraham with promises, Abraham "believed the LORD, and he counted it to him as righteousness" (Gen 15:6).

The Lord is continually promising blessing upon blessing to Abraham. Shortly after this promise of uncountable offspring, God makes a covenant of circumcision with Abraham. The Lord promises,

> I will establish my covenant between me and you and your offspring after you throughout their generations for an everlasting covenant, to be God for you and to your offspring after you...He who is eight days old among you shall be circumcised (Gen 17:7, 12).

This covenant identified God's people. It gave them a unique identity, setting them apart from other nations. On the eighth day, they were marked as God's chosen people. From Abraham's descendants would come the promised offspring who would crush the serpent's head. This sign connected them to the promised Christ, the one whose bright star would illuminate the way of the magi.

The apostle Paul writes that all these promises throughout the Old Testament find their fulfillment in Christ.[67] The covenant of circumcision ultimately finds its fulfillment in the work of Christ given in the sacrament of baptism.

In baptism, God fulfills his promise of being God for us. The reformer, Martin Luther, defines what it means for God to be for us in this way, "God, in turn, will be a God to them, that is, will do good to them in this life and in the eternal life, and will do all this because of Christ."[68] In baptism, God only does good for us on account of Christ.

---

[67] 2 Corinthians 1:20.

[68] Martin Luther, *Luther's Works, Volume 3*, gen. ed. Jaroslav Pelikan (Saint Louis: Concordia Publishing House, 1961), 92.

Through water and the Word, we are given a promise with no strings attached. We are brought into the everlasting covenant of forgiveness and life. The apostle Paul writes, "And you, who were dead in your trespasses and the uncircumcision of your flesh, God made alive together with him, having forgiven us all our trespasses" (Col 2:13). Just as God's people were given a new identity in the covenant of circumcision, so too we are given a new identity in our baptism.

This new identity as a baptized child of God can never be taken away from us. Our baptismal identity is a gift, a promise from our God who has promised to only bless us on account of Christ. It is a promise that our sins past, present, and future are all forgiven through water and the Word as we are dressed in the watery robes of Christ's righteousness in baptism.

This promise does not rely on us who waiver and doubt, but by our God who keeps his promise to us. Through the gift of the Holy Spirit, he keeps us in the faith, pointing us to the promises given to us, his baptized saints.

Heavenly Father, you have joined us to your Son in Holy Baptism. Through ordinary water connected to your almighty and gracious Word, you have gifted us with your Holy Spirit. Remember all your promises to us as we live as your baptized children, forgiven and sanctified through the work of your Son. Graciously bring us to daily repentance and forgive our sins according to your promise. Amen.

> **FOR FURTHER REFLECTION**
> **READ COLOSSIANS 3:1-17.**

WEEK FOUR

THE FIRST DAY OF THE FOURTH WEEK

Illuminated Waters

HE HAS DELIVERED US FROM THE DOMAIN OF DARKNESS AND TRANSFERRED US TO THE KINGDOM OF HIS BELOVED SON, IN WHOM WE HAVE REDEMPTION, THE FORGIVENESS OF SINS.

—Colossians 1:13-14

The apostle John opens his Gospel account with poetic imagery and language describing the second person of the Trinity, Jesus. John portrays him as the light that has come into the darkness of the world.

The word of God as light was a familiar image to John, whose Gospel was deeply rooted in the language and imagery of the Old Testament. From the Psalms[69] to the prophet Isaiah,[70] God's word shines on his people, bringing life and dispelling the darkness.

---
[69] Psalm 119:105.
[70] Isaiah 60:1-2.

The Lord is always bringing his people out of darkness and into his light. In the book of Exodus, God does this as he brings his people out of the darkness of slavery and into the light of the promised land.

Throughout the Old Testament, in the midst of his people's rebellion and sin, God is faithful to his promises; he keeps his word, despite the actions and sin of his people. The psalmist writes,

> For they had rebelled against the words of God, and spurned the counsel of the Most High... He brought them out of darkness and the shadow of death, and burst their bonds apart. Let them thank the LORD for his steadfast love, for his wondrous works to the children of man! (Ps 107:11, 14-15).

Jesus, the incarnate Word of God, "shines in the darkness, and the darkness has not overcome it" (John 1:5). Jesus came to bring life to a world darkened with the stain of sin. The Light of the world was born that he might absorb our darkness in his death.

As Jesus was crucified for us, the world plunged into darkness. The earth shook, rocks split, and the temple curtain was torn in two as the Light of the world was extinguished for our sin.[71]

But our darkness did not overcome him. Three days later, Jesus walked out of the darkness of his tomb, leaving behind our sins in his grave.

---

[71] Matthew 27:45, 51.

The apostle Paul writes that we have been delivered from a domain of darkness. Paul writes, "He has delivered us from the domain of darkness and transferred us to the kingdom of his beloved Son, in whom we have redemption, the forgiveness of sins" (Col 1:13-14).

God is the actor, the deliverer as we are plucked out of the kingdom of darkness and into the kingdom of Light, of his beloved Son. Just as God's people were passive as he delivered them from the darkness of slavery and sinful rebellion, so too are we passive in our deliverance from the domain of sin, death, and the power of the devil. Jesus does all the work, he delivers us.

In baptism, the Light of the world shines upon us, dispelling the darkness of our sin. Jesus delivers us from the domain of darkness in the name of the Father, Son, and Holy Spirit.

In many baptismal liturgies (or worship services) of the Christian church, the baptized is often given a candle which receives its light from the Paschal candle. Every year the baptized individual may light their baptismal candle and remember Christ, their light, who they received in baptism. As the candle burns bright and banishes the darkness, it recalls the light of Christ who has brought us into his glorious light of redemption.

The waters of our baptism are illumined with Christ, the light of the world. Through his wondrous works, he has delivered us from the domain of darkness. We now live in the kingdom of Christ, a kingdom without end, a kingdom in which the light of the Father's face is always shining upon us and blessing us because of what Christ has done for us.

Heavenly Father, you have washed our sins away in the flood of Holy Baptism. With water and your Word, you have joined us to your Son. Daily recall us to our baptism, where you promise to be faithful to all your gracious promises to us even when we are faithless. Forgive our sins and keep us in our baptismal faith through your Holy Spirit. Amen.

> **FOR FURTHER REFLECTION, READ PSALM 107.**

THE SECOND DAY OF THE FOURTH WEEK

The Final Word

AND AS THEY WERE FRIGHTENED AND BOWED THEIR FACES TO THE GROUND, THE MEN SAID TO THEM, "WHY DO YOU SEEK THE LIVING AMONG THE DEAD? HE IS NOT HERE, BUT HAS RISEN."

—Luke 24:5-6

The Sabbath had come and gone. As the sun rose on the eighth day, the women, loaded down with burial spices they had prepared, began their mournful journey to the tomb where Jesus had been laid.

As they approached the tomb, their plans to properly bury their beloved teacher and Lord were interrupted. Jesus was no longer in his tomb. The stone sealing his tomb had been rolled away. In the midst of their confusion, two angels, men in dazzling apparel, appeared and comforted the startled and astonished women, "Why do you seek the living among the dead? He is not here, but has risen" (Luke 24:5-6).

The women who had been overcome with grief, now returned to the disciples to share the good news. Their Lord was no longer dead, but alive-just as he had said.

Jesus' resurrection changes everything. The apostle Paul goes so far as to say Jesus' resurrection *is* everything and our faith hangs on this historical fact. Paul writes in his first letter to the church in Corinth, "And if Christ has not been raised, your faith is futile and you are still in your sins" (1 Cor 15:17).

If Jesus does not interrupt the pattern of death and walk out of his tomb, we would still be in our sins. We would be without hope if Christ had not been raised. Our baptism into Christ would have no power to save without the resurrection of our Lord into whose name we have been baptized.

But, thanks be to God, Christ is risen, he is risen indeed! Our faith is not futile but is alive and living because Jesus is alive and living. He has broken death's grip. Our Lord has left our sins behind in his dark tomb to be forever buried and forgotten.

The apostle Paul continues to unpack what Christ's resurrection means for us, as those who have been baptized. As one who has been baptized into Christ, he does not fear death. Rather, Paul quotes the prophets and with them, taunts death.

> "Death is swallowed up in victory. O death, where is your victory? O death, where is your sting?" The sting of death is sin, and the power

of sin is the law. But thanks be to God, who gives us the victory through our Lord Jesus Christ (1 Cor 15:54-55).

Death is swallowed up and drowned in the waters of baptism. Our sinful nature is drowned and buried in the watery tomb of the baptismal font. Our death will not have the final word. Jesus breaks the power and sting of death and has the final word in baptism.

In Christian funerals, there is a tradition of placing a white pall (or cloth) over the casket of the baptized saint. This tradition symbolizes the reality of the darkness of death being swallowed up by the bright white robe of Christ given in baptism. While we grieve those who have fallen asleep in Christ, the sting and power of death have been destroyed by our resurrected Lord. Death does not have the final word.

Through the water and the Word in baptism, we have been united to the One who is himself, we are carried by the working of the Holy Spirit on the waves of baptism to the shores of the resurrection.

Heavenly Father, you have washed our sins away in the flood of Holy Baptism. With water and your Word, you have joined us to your Son. Daily recall us to our baptism, where you promise to be faithful to all your gracious promises to us even when we are faithless. Forgive our sins and keep us in our baptismal faith through your Holy Spirit. Amen.

> **FOR FURTHER REFLECTION,**
> **READ 1 CORINTHIANS 15:1-28.**

THE THIRD DAY OF THE FOURTH WEEK

Still Waters

THE LORD IS MY SHEPHERD; I SHALL NOT WANT. HE MAKES ME LIE DOWN IN GREEN PASTURES. HE LEADS ME BESIDE STILL WATERS. HE RESTORES MY SOUL. HE LEADS ME IN PATHS OF RIGHTEOUSNESS FOR HIS NAME'S SAKE.

—Psalm 23:1-3

As a shepherd boy, the psalmist spent countless days and nights guarding his flock. David personally fought off predators that sought to devour his sheep. He knew firsthand of the stubborn, wayward, and helpless nature of his flock. And yet, this unruly, vulnerable, and rebellious animal is the illustration he chooses to describe himself in Psalm 23.

"The Lord is my shepherd," writes David. With these opening words of the psalm, he makes a confession. He confesses that he belongs to the Lord. He is under the merciful care and protection of the Lord, and he wants for nothing.

David continues, "He makes me lie down in green pastures. He leads me beside still waters. He restores my soul. He leads me in paths of righteousness for his name's sake" (Ps 23:2-3). As David paints with poetry, he creates an image of abundance, as baptismal waters flow through this psalm.

The shepherding David receives under the Lord's care is extraordinary. This shepherd not only sees to it that his sheep have green pastures and bountiful water, he restores his sheep. He abides with his flock and pursues his lost and wayward sheep, even at the cost of his own life.

Jesus picks up the imagery of Psalm 23 and says that he, himself, is our shepherd. Jesus said, "I came that they may have life and have it abundantly. I am the good shepherd. The good shepherd lays down his life for the sheep" (John 10:10-11). Not only does our Good Shepherd lead us to abundant life and still waters, he does so at the cost of laying down his life for sinful, stubborn, wandering sheep.

By the still waters of baptism, our Good Shepherd places his name upon us and restores our soul. He shepherds us with abundant care because he has made us his own. Our Good Shepherd abides with us even as we walk through the valley of the shadow of death.

Jesus is both our Good Shepherd and the Lamb of God who takes away our sin. As our good shepherd gave up his life into death for us. Out of the spear-pierced side of our sacrificial

Lamb flowed blood and water;[72] baptismal water that restores our soul, and his precious blood which he gives us along with his body to eat and drink in the sacrament of the Lord's Supper. There, he prepares a bountiful table for us in the presence of our foes.

The Lord is our shepherd. He has anointed us by the still waters of baptism where he has made us his own. There, he restores and resurrects our soul as we are united to Christ, the Lamb of God. Before us, he prepares a table of forgiveness, life, and salvation, even in the presence of our enemies of sin, death, and the devil. Our Good Shepherd comforts us with the rod of his cross and the staff of his Word. Surely, our Good Shepherd will abide with us and pursue us all the days of our life.

Heavenly Father, you have washed our sins away in the flood of Holy Baptism. With water and your Word, you have joined us to your Son. Daily recall us to our baptism, where you promise to be faithful to all your gracious promises to us even when we are faithless. Forgive our sins and keep us in our baptismal faith through your Holy Spirit. Amen.

FOR FURTHER REFLECTION, READ PSALM 23.

---

[72] John 19:34.

Drowned and Raised

BUT WHEN HE SAW THE WIND, HE WAS AFRAID, AND BEGINNING TO SINK HE CRIED OUT, "LORD, SAVE ME." JESUS IMMEDIATELY REACHED OUT HIS HAND AND TOOK HOLD OF HIM, SAYING TO HIM, "O YOU OF LITTLE FAITH, WHY DID YOU DOUBT?"

—Matthew 14:30-31

Water is a paradox. On one hand, it can be calm, peaceful, and life-giving, such as the still waters of Psalm 23. On the other hand, it can be devastating and violent, much like the flood waters in the book of Genesis.

It was not on the still waters, but rather on those violent, tempestuous, waters in which the disciples found themselves in Matthew's Gospel. As they crossed the Sea of Galilee at night, the waters churned around their boat. The wind whipped the water all around as they were violently rocked by the waves.

As they looked out into the stormy waters, they saw a ghost. They were sure of it and started to cry out in fear. In the midst of the howling sea was One who was walking on water. In response to their panicked cries, a familiar voice echoed across the water, "Take heart; it is I. Do not be afraid" (Matt 14:27).

The sight of one walking on water brings the words of the Old Testament book of Job to mind. Job describes God in this way, as One, "who alone stretched out the heavens and trampled the waves of the sea" (Job 9:8).

The Word made flesh, the One who created all things and sustains all things, now walked on the chaotic sea with authority as if it were solid ground.

Peter wastes no time. He knows his shepherd's voice. He called out as the storm raged, "Lord, if it is you, command me to come to you on the water" (Matt 14:28). Step by step, Peter began walking on water toward his Lord. But, as the wind raged around him, he became afraid and started sinking.

Peter cried out, "Lord, save me" (Matt 14:30). Just as Peter's ability to walk on the water came from the external word of Jesus, so too his rescue must come from the external Word.

Jesus did not waste a moment. He immediately reached out his hand and took hold of Peter. Jesus said to him, "O you of little faith, why did you doubt?" (Matt 14:31). As Jesus and Peter returned to the boat, the sea suddenly became calm.

Just as Jesus' voice echoed across the sea that night, so too his voice echoes across the waters of baptism. As the world rages around us our Lord calls to us, "Take heart; it is I. Do not be afraid."

The one who tramples the waves of the sea, saves us in the waters of baptism. Just as Peter relied on an external word and action from Jesus, so too we rely on the external word and action of Jesus for us. We do not baptize ourselves by our own strength. The actor alone is the Word who grabs hold of us with his outstretched, nail scarred hands.

We are daily returned to our baptism in repentance. As Peter sank in the water and was raised by the hand of the Lord, so too, our sinful nature is drowned in the waters of baptism, and we are raised to new life in Christ who has grabbed us with his mighty Word.

We are kept by the external Word who called out to us, who grabbed hold of us, and who keeps us by the working of the Holy Spirit in our baptismal faith. Jesus said, "I give them eternal life, and they will never perish, and no one will snatch them out of my hand. My Father, who has given them to me, is greater than all, and no one is able to snatch them out of the Father's hand" (John 10:28-29).

We who are baptized into Christ are a paradox. We are sinners and saints at the same time. In baptism, we are drowned and die to sin, while at the same time, are raised to new life in Christ.

Baptism is a promise from our Lord who walks on water, and calms the wind, that we are safe in him. Our sins are forgiven, washed away, and buried in the baptismal font.

Heavenly Father, you have washed our sins away in the flood of Holy Baptism. With water and your Word, you have joined us to your Son. Daily recall us to our baptism, where you promise to be faithful to all your gracious promises to us even when we are faithless. Forgive our sins and keep us in our baptismal faith through your Holy Spirit. Amen.

> **FOR FURTHER REFLECTION,
> READ MATTHEW 14:22-33.**

What Debt?

IF YOU, O LORD, SHOULD MARK INIQUITIES, O LORD, WHO COULD STAND? BUT WITH YOU THERE IS FORGIVENESS, THAT YOU MAY BE FEARED. I WAIT FOR THE LORD, MY SOUL WAITS, AND IN HIS WORD I HOPE.

—Psalm 130:3-5

In his Gospel account, Matthew records a parable Jesus told of a king who wished to settle accounts. Matthew, a former tax collector, knew all about debts and keeping track of what people owed, given his background.

He had made a career of tracking debts. Tucked away within the confines of his tax booth, he tallied up accounts and demanded payment. His life was engrossed with bookkeeping. As a tax collector, Matthew's life revolved around making sure every last debt was settled.

Jesus continues his parable with the king uncovering the magnitude of debt one of his servants owed. It was a debt so astronomically large; it was impossible to even begin to pay back. The servant has nothing to offer his master. He does not seem to even fully grasp the magnitude of his debt as he pleads for patience from his king, promising to pay it all back.

The psalmist ponders the consequences if the Lord kept a record of our sins. What would happen if the Lord kept a ledger, marking our sins one by one? The psalmist writes, "If you, O LORD, should mark iniquities, O Lord, who could stand?" (Ps 130:3). If the Lord kept a record of our sins, we would be like the servant in Jesus' parable, owing a debt we could never pay back.

The king, however, was determined to settle accounts. The servant would not be sent away with an outstanding balance. The king will not grant his servant more time to pay. To everyone's surprise, the king just settles the balance himself and closes the ledger.

By forgiving the debt of his servant, the king claimed the servant's debt as his own. The debt no longer belonged to the servant. This illustration, Jesus says, is a picture of the kingdom of heaven.

Just like the king in the parable, Jesus has come to settle accounts. Jesus is not merely patient with us while we, oblivious to the magnitude of our sin, ask for more time to pay back our debt—he personally takes on our astronomical debt of sin as his own. He carries our ledger heavy with the ink of our sin up to mount calvary.

In his death, Jesus settled the debt we owed. As the temple curtain was torn in two as Jesus died,[73] the ledger and record of our sin was torn up and destroyed as well. Our debt is fully forgiven, personally paid in full by our King, himself.

The psalmist, after pondering the possible outcome of the Lord tallying up our account of sin, swiftly finishes his thought with the proclamation of praise. The psalmist writes, "But with you there is forgiveness, that you may be feared. I wait for the LORD, my soul waits, and in his word I hope" (Ps 130:4-5).

In baptism, our debts are forgiven. Through water and God's word our debt is wiped out. Page by page the ledger of our sin (past, present, and future) dissolves in the waters of baptism. The theologian Robert Farrar Capon writes,

> "We are forgiven in baptism not only for the sins committed before baptism but for a whole lifetime of sins yet to come. We are forgiven before, during, and after our sins. And we are forgiven for one reason only: because Jesus died for our sins and rose for our justification."[74]

Before God, we have no record of sin. The Lord remembers our sins no more.[75] In fact, we are given a new ledger in baptism.

---

[73] Matthew 27:51.

[74] Robert Farrar Capon, *Kingdom, Grace, Judgment: Paradox, Outrage, and Vindication in the Parables of Jesus* (Grand Rapids, MI: William B. Eerdmans Publishing Company, 2002), 297.

[75] Hebrews 8:12.

Instead of being saturated with the weight of our sin, this one is saturated with works of Christ for us.

We are baptized. Jesus' perfect record has our names on it. Our Heavenly Father has sent his only Son to take care of our debt in his death and resurrection. Now, wealthy with the righteousness of Christ, we are free to dispense forgiveness as if it was limitless.

Heavenly Father, you have washed our sins away in the flood of Holy Baptism. With water and your Word, you have joined us to your Son. Daily recall us to our baptism, where you promise to be faithful to all your gracious promises to us even when we are faithless. Forgive our sins and keep us in our baptismal faith through your Holy Spirit. Amen.

> **FOR FURTHER REFLECTION,**
> **READ MATTHEW 18:21-35.**

Splashing in Baptismal Waters

BUT WHEN JESUS SAW IT, HE WAS INDIGNANT AND SAID TO THEM, "LET THE CHILDREN COME TO ME; DO NOT HINDER THEM, FOR TO SUCH BELONGS THE KINGDOM OF GOD."

—Mark 10:14

Jesus is known for his patience, kindness, and mercy. Wherever he went, Jesus healed the sick and preached the good news of the kingdom of God. He drove out demons and made outcasts whole again. He even distributed forgiveness to sinners recklessly, as though it was his sole possession to offer.

Jesus' patience is unmatched. He is slow to anger and abounding in love. However, all three synoptic Gospel writers, Matthew, Mark, and Luke record an account of where

Jesus becomes indignant with his disciples. Jesus becomes angered when his disciples hinder little children from coming to him.

> But when Jesus saw it, he was indignant and said to them, "Let the children come to me; do not hinder them, for to such belongs the kingdom of God. Truly, I say to you, whoever does not receive the kingdom of God like a child shall not enter it" (Mark 10:14-15).

These little children, seemingly interrupting the work of Jesus' ministry, were in fact the epitome of those to whom the kingdom of God belongs.

They had nothing to offer or contribute. These little ones could only receive a blessing from their Lord. They could only say, "amen," to the gifts of God. They had no money to contribute to his ministry, no experience to offer, and yet they are those to whom the kingdom of God belongs. In hindering the children from their Lord, the disciples were hindering those to whom Jesus seeks to love and show mercy and love.

In the waters of Holy Baptism, we receive the kingdom of God as a child receives a gift. The kingdom of God is not dependent on our works, contributions, or our understanding. Like a little child, we humbly say "amen" as we receive the gifts and promises of God given in baptism.

It is there, in the waters of baptism, where we become children of God. Through baptism, we receive the kingdom of God, a kingdom in which our sins are washed away, and we receive all the good and gracious gifts of the Father, Son, and Holy Spirit.

Our Lord deals by means of promises and gifts. We enter the kingdom of God as those who can only receive everything from our Heavenly Father. The kingdom of God is completely one-sided. Though we have nothing but our sin to offer, our Heavenly Father scoops us up in the baptismal waters and washes our sin away. He then clothes us with the gift of righteousness from his beloved Son.

After we have received these gifts given in our baptism, we do not outgrow and leave behind the waters of our baptism. Rather, we swim deeper into these baptismal gifts, splashing like a little child in the gifting, saving, Word-soaked waters. Through baptism, we receive a gracious Heavenly Father who cares for us. As baptized children, we grab hold of him and his promises with confidence, as a child interacts with their gracious father. We look to Christ to clean up our sin, as we turn to our Heavenly Father through daily repentance.

We have been received into the kingdom of God as little children through baptism, through the work of Jesus for us. The Father, Son, and Holy Spirit have promised to keep us in this gift-receiving life, held securely in his baptismal grace.

Heavenly Father, you have washed our sins away in the flood of Holy Baptism. With water and your Word, you have joined us to your Son. Daily recall us to our baptism, where you promise to be faithful to all your gracious promises to us even when we are faithless. Forgive our sins and keep us in our baptismal faith through your Holy Spirit. Amen.

FOR FURTHER REFLECTION, READ MARK 10:13-16.

A Sanctified Bath

BUT YOU WERE WASHED, YOU WERE SANCTIFIED, YOU WERE JUSTIFIED IN THE NAME OF THE LORD JESUS CHRIST AND BY THE SPIRIT OF OUR GOD.

—1 Corinthians 6:11

In the middle of the apostle Paul's letter to the church in Corinth, he pauses to remind the Corinthians what God has done for them. Amidst addressing all of the idolatry, sin, and divisions within the Corinthian church, Paul begins with, and continually returns to what God in Christ has accomplished for them.

The apostle has some harsh words for the Corinthians. After reproaching them, Paul gives this stern warning, "or do you not know that the unrighteous will not inherit the kingdom of God?" (1 Cor. 6:9). Sinners have no place in the kingdom of God apart from Christ.

The saints in Corinth, however, are not the only ones battling their sinful nature. The apostle, himself, writes of his own struggle with sin,

> For I delight in the law of God, in my inner being, but I see in my members another law waging war against the law of my mind and making me captive to the law of sin that dwells in my members. Wretched man that I am! Who will deliver me from this body of death? Thanks be to God through Jesus Christ our Lord! (Rom 7:22-25).

The church in Corinth, the apostle Paul, and we have no place in the kingdom of God, that is, apart from Christ. Immediately following Paul's warning of the consequences of sin, he reminds the church of their sanctification. We cannot make ourselves righteous, we cannot sanctify or justify ourselves.

But thanks be to God! Through Holy Baptism, we have been bathed with water and the Word. We are sanctified and justified as the name of our Lord is placed upon us in baptism. In this baptismal bath, our sins are washed away, and we are declared justified in the name of our Lord Jesus Christ and given the gift of the Holy Spirit to believe.

After being washed in the sanctifying waters of baptism, however, our sinful nature goes forth and daily walks around in the mud of sin. Through the gift of the Holy Spirit, we are daily turned back to our baptism, back to where God promised to wash off all our dirt and sin.

The baptized life is a sanctified life. It is a life in which God daily and richly repents us. To say, "I am baptized," is to live in repentance and the gifts of Christ. It is to say, "all God's promises are for me; in my baptism, he has promised me the forgiveness of all my sins and life everlasting. He has made me his beloved child and has promised to keep me in Christ, into whose name I have been baptized."

Sanctification is to make something holy, and through baptism, we have been placed united with the holy Son of God. In his commentary on the book of Romans, theologian Jonathan F. Grothe writes,

> "Your sanctification, which *God* is seeing to, has begun with Christ's death and your baptism. It continues every present moment as you live in the Holy Christian Church in which God daily and richly forgives sins."[76]

Sanctification comes through hearing the gospel proclaimed, of Christ's death and resurrection for you. In the absolution, we receive the forgiveness of all our sins, the same forgiveness given to us in our baptism. Through these gospel gift, our sinful nature is drowned, and we rise to new life in Christ.

Baptism is sanctification, it is where we are made holy. It is where God is at work for you. We cannot sanctify ourselves,

---

[76] Jonathan F. Grothe, *Justification of the Ungodly: An Interpretation of Romans*, 2nd ed. (Ontario, Canada, St. Catherines, 2012), 336.

but thanks be to God! Through the sanctifying bath of baptism, our sins are washed away, and we are made holy, in the name of our Lord Jesus Christ and by the Spirit of our God.

Heavenly Father, you have washed our sins away in the flood of Holy Baptism. With water and your Word, you have joined us to your Son. Daily recall us to our baptism, where you promise to be faithful to all your gracious promises to us even when we are faithless. Forgive our sins and keep us in our baptismal faith through your Holy Spirit. Amen.

> **FOR FURTHER REFLECTION, READ ROMANS 7:7-25.**

Called by Name

JESUS SAID TO HER, "DO NOT CLING TO ME, FOR I HAVE NOT YET ASCENDED TO THE FATHER; BUT GO TO MY BROTHERS AND SAY TO THEM, I AM ASCENDING TO MY FATHER AND YOUR FATHER, TO MY GOD AND YOUR GOD."

—John 20:17

Mary, overwhelmed by grief, did not recognize him. It had been three days since she witnessed the dreadful suffering and death of her beloved teacher and friend. As Mary stood weeping outside the tomb where Jesus had been laid, her grief was interrupted by who she could only have presumed to be the gardener.

> Jesus said to her, "Woman, why are you weeping? Whom are you seeking?" Supposing him to be the gardener, she said to him, "Sir if you have carried him away, tell me where you have laid him, and I will take him away" (John 20:15).

In her profound sorrow, Mary failed to recognize Jesus, the very One she was grieving, as he stood before her and addressed her. Then, with one word, her resurrected Lord opened her eyes.

> Jesus said to her, 'Mary.' She turned and said to him in Aramaic, 'Rabboni!' (which means Teacher) (John 20:16).

The Good Shepherd, after laying down his life, fervently pursued his sheep. After his resurrection from the dead, Jesus sought out Mary to interrupt her despair and bring her comfort.

Jesus opened Mary's eyes as he called her by name. Mary's tears of grief were turned to tears of gladness and joy. Jesus, who was once dead, is now risen. He is risen, indeed!

But then, something strange happens.

Jesus told Mary not to cling to him. Jesus instructs her to return to his disciples. He directs Mary to return with this message, "I am ascending to my Father and your Father, to my God and your God" (John 20:17).

For forty days after his resurrection, Jesus walked the earth, teaching and instructing his disciples. In those days of instruction, Jesus gave his disciples the authority to forgive sins.[77] He instituted the sacrament of Holy Baptism as he commanded his disciples to go out and baptize all nations in the name of the Father, Son, and Holy Spirit.[78] Jesus spent those forty days

---
[77] John 20:22-23.
[78] Matthew 28:19.

after his resurrection teaching his disciples to observe all he had commanded them.

Jesus then ascended just as he had told Mary. But he is not gone. He promised he would be with us always.[79] Jesus may be hidden from our earthly eyes, but he is at work among us.

Jesus directed Mary to where he would be with her and for her. In his church and through the preaching and teaching of his disciples, Jesus would be for Mary. Through the proclamation of the gospel and the giving of his gifts, Jesus would be at work for her.

Just as Mary was left in the care of Jesus' disciples, so too, we are left in the care of the church in which Jesus is present and at work for us. Through the work of our pastor, Jesus comforts our troubled consciences with the forgiveness of sins in the absolution. Through the sacrament of the altar, the Lord feeds us his body and blood for the forgiveness of our sins.

In baptism, our Good Shepherd has called us by name. Our resurrected Lord comforts us through his gospel. Jesus has grabbed hold of us in our baptism and will not let us go.

Heavenly Father, you have washed our sins away in the flood of Holy Baptism. With water and your Word, you have joined us to

---

[79] Matthew 28:20.

your Son. Daily recall us to our baptism, where you promise to be faithful to all your gracious promises to us even when we are faithless. Forgive our sins and keep us in our baptismal faith through your Holy Spirit. Amen.

> **FOR FURTHER REFLECTION, READ JOHN 10:1-18.**

WEEK FIVE

THE FIRST DAY OF THE FIFTH WEEK

Baptized into the Promised Land

NOW THE PRIESTS BEARING THE ARK OF THE COVENANT OF THE LORD STOOD FIRMLY ON DRY GROUND IN THE MIDST OF THE JORDAN, AND ALL ISRAEL WAS PASSING OVER ON DRY GROUND UNTIL ALL THE NATION FINISHED PASSING OVER THE JORDAN.

—Joshua 3:17

The children of Israel stood on the banks of the Jordan river overlooking the promised land. The Lord had brought them to this crossing. After he powerfully and miraculously rescued his people from the hands of their Egyptian captors, he led them on dry ground through the Red Sea as he drowned their foes. And now, after forty years of wandering in the wilderness (grumbling all the way), he would lead them again through water.

God kept all of his promises to them. In the wilderness, he provided manna from heaven,[80] quail for meat,[81] and water from a rock.[82] During those forty years in the wilderness, despite their unbelief and rebellious grumbling hearts, the Lord was merciful and patient with his people.

Now, Israel gathered on the banks of the Jordan river to cross into the fulfillment of the Lord's promise to them.[83] The Lord appointed Joshua to lead his people into the promised land. As they prepared to cross, the priests went out before the people carrying the ark of the covenant, representing God's presence among his people. Then, as the feet of the priests carrying the ark hit the water of the Jordan, the flow of water was miraculously held back.

Just as Israel had crossed the Red Sea on dry ground as they fled Egypt, so too they crossed through the water of the Jordan River on dry ground to receive the land promised to them. The ark of the covenant held by the priests stood firm in the midst of the river as Israel passed through.

This miraculous crossing took place in the same river in which John the baptizer would one day cry out along its banks, "Prepare the way of the Lord" (Matt 3:3). Just as the ark of the covenant stood in the midst of the river, so Jesus stood firm in

---

[80] Exodus 16:4.
[81] Exodus 16:12.
[82] Exodus 17:6.
[83] Exodus 6:8.

the midst of the Jordan River as he was baptized for us. Then, as Jesus came up from the water, "behold, the heavens were opened to him, and he saw the Spirit of God descending like a dove and coming to rest on him" (Matt 3:16).

As the waters were held back for Israel, so too the flood waters of God's wrath are held back from us in Christ. He stands in our place, holding back the wrath of God for our sin, taking it upon himself. Jesus is our greater Joshua. It is Jesus (whose name translates to Joshua in Hebrew) who leads us into the promised land of a new heavens and a new earth.

In our baptism, we receive the promises of God. Through water and the Word, we pass over from death to life. The apostle Paul writes, "Therefore, if anyone is in Christ, he is a new creation. The old has passed away; behold, the new has come" (2 Cor 5:17). Just as Israel passed from the wilderness to the land God promised them by the Lord's hand, so too, we pass from the wilderness of sin and death to the promise of forgiveness and everlasting life, by the Lord's hand in baptism.

God keeps his promises to us. As we wander through this earthly wilderness awaiting the resurrection, the Lord is merciful to us and provides for all our needs. He has provided life from baptismal water flowing from the side of the Rock of Christ.[84] He feeds us in the Lord's Supper with the manna which has come

---

[84] 1 Corinthians 10:4.

down from heaven, the very body and blood of our Lord for the forgiveness of our sins.[85]

Jesus, our Joshua, leads us into the abundant land of forgiveness and life. Through our baptism into Christ, we have received the salvation of the Lord.

Heavenly Father, you have baptized us and placed us into the care of your church. You have given us the gift of your Holy Spirit. Sanctify us as we cling to the promises you have gifted us in baptism. Keep us safe in the ark of Christ and of your church that we may safely reach the shores of the resurrection, where we will finally see the fulfillment of all your promises to us with our own eyes. Amen.

> **FOR FURTHER REFLECTION, READ JOSHUA 3:1-17.**

---

[85] John 6:48-51.

A Naval Church

THEY WENT INTO THE ARK WITH NOAH, TWO AND TWO OF ALL FLESH IN WHICH THERE WAS THE BREATH OF LIFE. AND THOSE THAT ENTERED, MALE AND FEMALE OF ALL FLESH, WENT IN AS GOD HAD COMMANDED HIM. AND THE LORD SHUT HIM IN.

—Genesis 7:15-16

The architecture and articles within Christian churches for centuries have echoed the narrative of the flood, linking the Genesis narrative to the sacrament of Holy Baptism. The building and articles therein served to point its worshipers to the saving work of Christ in baptism.

The Lord sent a flood to destroy the world because of the wickedness of mankind, Moses writes in the book of Genesis chapters six and seven. Noah, however found favor with God. He believed God's word. And, because of the

Lord's promise to him, he, along with his family, were spared as they entered the safety of the ark.[86]

Noah built this ark according to the Lord's instructions. As Noah entered the ark with his family and all the creatures, the Lord shut them in. The earth burst and the water rained down, lifting the ark to safety. The eight souls aboard were kept safe from God's watery judgment against sin and unbelief. As the waters raged and killed all wicked mankind, Noah and his family remained safe inside the ark, the vehicle by which God chose to save them.

The apostle Peter references this account in his epistle.[87] He writes that the flood was a foreshadowing of how we are saved through the water and Word in baptism. The ark, which safely held the congregation of eight souls on the water, is an illustration of the church of Christ.

Many baptismal fonts contain eight sides for this reason. Through baptism, we are placed, together with all the saints, into the ark of Christ. We are saved by God's promise through water and his Word. Baptism is the means (or vehicle) by which God gives his saving gifts of the forgiveness of sins and everlasting life.

Baptism is also the means by which God kills our sinful nature. Our sinful unbelief is drowned in this baptismal flood. In his

---

[86] Genesis 6:18-19.
[87] 1 Peter 3:20-21.

baptismal liturgy, the reformer, Martin Luther wrote a prayer in which he prays that in the waters of baptism, our Lord would drown our sinful nature and keep us safe in the ark of the church. Luther writes,

> ...by means of this saving flood all that has been born in him from Adam and which he himself has added thereto may be drowned in him and engulfed, and that he may be sundered from the number of the unbelieving, preserved dry and secure in the holy ark of Christendom.[88]

The architecture of many churches resembles that of an upside-down boat or ark. The building confesses that here, in the ark of the church, the gospel of Christ's saving work for us is preached, and his life-giving gifts are delivered in Word and sacrament. In baptism, we are brought into this ark of the church, and of Christ, that we might be safe from God's righteous judgment for our sins.

The account of the flood is an illustration of what God has done and is doing for us, the baptized. God continually drowns and puts to death our sinful nature, while at the same time securing us in the ark of Christ.

We have found favor in the eyes of God. Not because of our works, but because of his mercy and promise in baptism. We

---

[88] Martin Luther, *Luther's Works: Liturgy and Hymns*, vol. 53, ed. Ulrich S. Leupold (Philadelphia, PA: Fortress Press, 1965), 107-108.

are righteous in the eyes of God as we are held in the embrace of Christ, our ark.

Heavenly Father, you have baptized us and placed us into the care of your church. You have given us the gift of your Holy Spirit. Sanctify us as we cling to the promises you have gifted us in baptism. Keep us safe in the ark of Christ and of your church that we may safely reach the shores of the resurrection, where we will finally see the fulfillment of all your promises to us with our own eyes. Amen.

> **FOR FURTHER REFLECTION, READ GENESIS 7:1-24.**

THE THIRD DAY OF THE FIFTH WEEK

Parched Bones

SO I PROPHESIED AS HE COMMANDED
ME, AND THE BREATH CAME INTO THEM,
AND THEY LIVED AND STOOD ON THEIR FEET,
AN EXCEEDINGLY GREAT ARMY.

—Ezekiel 37:10

This account from the prophet Ezekiel unfolds like a sci-fi film. The prophet is led to an eerie valley littered with brittle, parched, dried-up bones, void of life. These brittle bones were beyond revival. And yet, the Lord asks Ezekiel if these bones can live. The Lord follows up his question by telling Ezekiel to speak the word of the Lord over the bones.

> O dry bones, hear the word of the LORD. Thus says the Lord GOD to these bones: Behold, I will cause breath to enter you, and you shall live. And I will lay sinews upon you, and will cause flesh to come upon you, and cover you with skin, and put breath in you, and you shall live, and you shall know that I am the LORD (Ezek 37:4-6).

Ezekiel prophesied as the Lord commanded. Then, the prophet watched in awe as the valley began to rattle and vibrate with the sound of these dusty, skeletal remains snapping together. Death began dissipating as the eerie sound of bones coming together one by one filled the valley. Tendons emerged sewing together muscle and bone. Flesh started rapidly knitting itself together as death vacated the valley.

The unthinkable, and unimaginable, played out like a scene from a movie, before the prophet's eyes. But there was still one problem. While the bones now had the appearance of life, they remain dead, void of any breath. The Lord again told his prophet to speak to them:

> Thus says the Lord GOD: Come from the four winds, O breath, and breathe on these slain, that they may live (Ezek 37:9).

As Ezekiel spoke, breath came into them. What was once a pile of dry, dead bones, was now an immensely large, resurrected, living, breathing army. God's word, spoken by his prophet, brought these brittle, death-ridden bones back to life. Death had been overtaken by God's word.

We were like the dead bones in that desolate valley. And not just a little dead, but dead dead. We were as far from life as those dry, parched, bones, turning to dust. The apostle Paul writes, "you were dead in the trespasses and sins in which you once walked... But God, being rich in mercy, because of the great love with which he loved us, even when we were dead in our trespasses, made us alive together with Christ" (Eph 2:1-2, 4-5).

Just as God's word brought these parched bones back to life, his Word also imparts life to us in baptism. The Word speaks us back to life. Our parched bones are hydrated by the water and God's word in baptism.

A miracle happens as we are resurrected in this sacrament. The breath of the Holy Spirit enters the baptized, and the Lord takes our heart of stone and gives us a heart of flesh.[89] Baptism brings us out of the parched valley of dry bones and into the luscious green pastures of Psalm 23.

The baptismal life is a new life hydrated by the word of God and gift of the Holy Spirit. As we daily return to our baptism in repentance, we recall the promise of Lord, "I will save them from all the backslidings in which they have sinned and will cleanse them; and they shall be my people, and I will be their God" (Ezek 37:23).

Our baptism isn't a work in which we muster up enough faith and commitment to prove our allegiance to the Lord. Baptism is solely the work of the Lord as he water and Words us back to life in the name of the Father, and of the Son, and of the Holy Spirit. It is a gracious gift we receive as our dead bones rattle back to life through the forgiveness of sins. Our Lord abides

---

[89] Ezekiel 36:26.

with his Christian church, an immensely large army of baptized saints, to escort us through the valley of the shadow of death, into life everlasting and the resurrection of the dead.

Heavenly Father, you have baptized us and placed us into the care of your church. You have given us the gift of your Holy Spirit. Sanctify us as we cling to the promises you have gifted us in baptism. Keep us safe in the ark of Christ and of your church that we may safely reach the shores of the resurrection, where we will finally see the fulfillment of all your promises to us with our own eyes. Amen.

> **FOR FURTHER REFLECTION, READ EZEKIEL 37:1-28.**

THE FOURTH DAY OF THE FIFTH WEEK

Our Great High Priest

NOW JOSHUA WAS STANDING BEFORE THE ANGEL, CLOTHED WITH FILTHY GARMENTS. AND THE ANGEL SAID TO THOSE WHO WERE STANDING BEFORE HIM, "REMOVE THE FILTHY GARMENTS FROM HIM." AND TO HIM HE SAID, "BEHOLD, I HAVE TAKEN YOUR INIQUITY AWAY FROM YOU, AND I WILL CLOTHE YOU WITH PURE VESTMENTS."

—Zechariah 3:3-4

As Israel returned from their Babylonian captivity, Zechariah was a prophet among God's people. He called the Lord's people to repentance and encouraged the rebuilding of the temple. Among the prophet Zechariah's writings, eight visions are recorded. The fourth of which depicts a striking interaction between Satan, the angel of the Lord, and Joshua the high priest.

The vision unfolds with Satan, the accuser, standing at the ready to throw accusations at Joshua, the high priest. Joshua, clothed with filthy garments, does not utter a word. The angel of the Lord, however, speaks up and rebukes Satan.

The angel then demands the filthy garments be removed from Joshua and has him clothed with pure vestments and a clean turban. He then addresses Joshua and says, "Behold, I have taken your iniquity away from you, and I will clothe you with pure vestments" (Zech 3:4).

As the high priest, Joshua represented all Israel. The high priest's garments were sacred, intricately woven, and included a chest plate with the names of all the tribes of Israel. The high priest's job was to intercede for the people and offer sacrifices in the temple to atone for their sin.

However, as Joshua stands before the angel of the Lord, the accuser at his side, he is not dressed in his regal priestly garments. He is dressed in filthy garments. He is dressed in the sins of Israel. The prophet Isaiah writes, "We have all become like one who is unclean, and all our righteous deeds are like a polluted garment" (Isa 64:6).

This vision of Zechariah foreshadows the work of our greater high priest in baptism. Our greater high priest shares the same name, Joshua, which is Jesus in Greek. As our Great High Priest, Jesus intercedes for us. He does not offer animal sacrifices in the temple. He, himself, the holy Lamb of God, gives his life as a sacrifice. He, himself, is the atonement for our sin.

Zechariah continues with the words of the Lord, "I will bring my servant the Branch...I will remove the iniquity of this land in a single day" (Zech 3:8, 9). This Branch is Christ who would remove the iniquity of the sins of the world on a single day. Jesus, the Branch, removed our iniquities as he hung on the tree of his cross. As he cried, "It is finished," (John 19:30) he silenced our accuser.

Our Joshua takes our filthy garments upon himself and gives us his pure vestments in baptism. The apostle Paul writes, "For as many of you as were baptized into Christ have put on Christ" (Gal 3:27). In baptism, this great exchange takes place. The theologian, Robert Farrar Capon, describes baptism in this way,

> "In baptism we are clothed, once and for all, with a forgiveness woven for us by Jesus' death and resurrection."[90]

In baptism, Jesus interrupts the accusations of Satan against us and redirects them toward calvary. Our sin has been paid in full. Our guilt has been removed through water and God's word. Our filthy garments have been taken away and we are now clothed with Christ. We belong to Christ and Satan cannot accuse us anymore. We are baptized into Christ!

---

[90] Robert Farrar Capon, *Kingdom, Grace, Judgment: Paradox, Outrage, and Vindication in the Parables of Jesus* (Grand Rapids, MI: William B. Eerdmans Publishing Company, 2002), 193.

Heavenly Father, you have baptized us and placed us into the care of your church. You have given us the gift of your Holy Spirit. Sanctify us as we cling to the promises you have gifted us in baptism. Keep us safe in the ark of Christ and of your church that we may safely reach the shores of the resurrection, where we will finally see the fulfillment of all your promises to us with our own eyes. Amen.

> **FOR FURTHER REFLECTION,
> READ ZECHARIAH 3:1-10.**

Anointed

AND IT IS GOD WHO ESTABLISHES US WITH YOU IN CHRIST, AND HAS ANOINTED US, AND WHO HAS ALSO PUT HIS SEAL ON US AND GIVEN US HIS SPIRIT IN OUR HEARTS AS A GUARANTEE.

—2 Corinthians 1:21-22

The Lord set apart his chosen ones in the Old Testament by anointing them. Priests, kings, and prophets were sought out by the Lord to receive an anointing with oil. This event was a tangible, historical anointing, which left no doubt that this individual was consecrated to the Lord.

In second Corinthians, the apostle Paul elaborates on our anointing. He writes that we have been anointed by God. We have a seal placed upon us and are given his Spirit. But how does this happen?

Through the water and God's word in baptism, all this takes place. In Holy Baptism, we are set apart and sought out by the Lord and anointed, not with oil, but with water and his word. Here, God anoints us and establishes us in Christ. The Spirit is given to us in baptism as a guarantee of our salvation.

In our baptism, we too have a tangible, historical event in which we are consecrated to the Lord as his beloved saint, a dearly loved child of our Heavenly Father. The Lord sought us out in our baptism to give us his gifts. We have been given baptism as a historical, tangible event, in which we can look to and know that we belong to Christ, our sins are forgiven, and we will rise with all the saints in the resurrection.

The Spirit given to us, anchors us firmly in our baptismal waters as he holds up Christ and his work for us. Jesus says of the Spirit, "But when the Helper comes, whom I will send to you from the Father, the Spirit of truth, who proceeds from the Father, he will bear witness about me" (John 15:26).

The Spirit is given to us as a guarantee that our sins are forgiven. He bears witness that Jesus took the wages of our sin as he hung on the tree of life for us. The Spirit recalls to us our baptism where we receive the fruits of Jesus' labor. Through saving water and the Word, we are established in him who is the Resurrection and the Life. The Spirit guarantees that Christ's righteousness has been given to us, and our sin remains buried and forgotten in his tomb.

The apostle Paul writes, "But God's firm foundation stands, bearing this seal: 'The Lord knows those who are his'" (2 Tim 2:19).

We have this seal upon us in our baptism. We are known by our Lord, and our Good Shepherd calls us by name.

In baptism, the Trinity takes hold of us and puts his seal upon us. When waves of doubt threaten us, we can look to our baptism, a historical event in our lives, in which the Holy Trinity called us by name and united us with Christ.

In light of this, we can boldly proclaim, "I am baptized!" We have been anointed in the waters of baptism and can find assurance in this watery anointing. We can take comfort in the Lord's words from the prophet Isaiah,

> But now thus says the LORD, he who created you, O Jacob, he who formed you, O Israel: Fear not, for I have redeemed you; I have called you by name, you are mine (Isa 43:1).

Jesus has finished everything for our redemption. He has called us by name and claimed us in this blessed gift of baptism. Jesus has taken our sin away and gives us his life and righteousness. We are his. There is nothing left for us to do. It is all a merciful gift from the Father, Son, and Holy Spirit.

Heavenly Father, you have baptized us and placed us into the care of your church. You have given us the gift of your Holy Spirit. Sanctify us as we cling to the promises you have gifted us in baptism. Keep us safe in the ark of Christ and of your church that we may safely reach the shores of the resurrection, where we will finally see the fulfillment of all your promises to us with our own eyes. Amen.

> **FOR FURTHER REFLECTION,
> READ EPHESIANS 1:1-23.**

THE SIXTH DAY OF THE FIFTH WEEK

The River of Life

BUT ONE OF THE SOLDIERS PIERCED HIS SIDE WITH A SPEAR, AND AT ONCE THERE CAME OUT BLOOD AND WATER.

—*John 19:34*

John begins as the book of Genesis begins. Unlike the Gospels of Matthew, Mark, and Luke, he does not begin with the birth of Christ or a genealogy leading up to the birth of Christ. Instead, he goes back to the beginning, back to the creation.

> In the beginning was the Word, and the Word was with God, and the Word was God. He was in the beginning with God. All things were made through him, and without him was not anything made that was made (John 1:1-3).

John weaves the narrative of Genesis into the fabric of his Gospel account. With the opening of his Gospel, he establishes Jesus as the Word of the Father. Through Jesus all things were created.

As John records the passion of our Lord, he does not move away from this Genesis narrative. He spills far more ink in the details surrounding Jesus' death than any other Gospel account. Yet, even in his death, Jesus is the means through which all things are made anew.

The apostle John has a unique perspective as he recalls the death of Jesus. While all the disciples scattered as Jesus was taken in the garden, John stood alongside Jesus' mother and watched as his Lord was crucified. It is there, in his eye-witness testimony from Calvary, in which John records this small, seemingly insignificant detail. "But one of the soldiers pierced his side with a spear, and at once there came out blood and water" (John 19:34).

As Jesus fell into the deep sleep of death, after finishing the work of our salvation, a Roman soldier pierced his side. From the side of Christ flowed his blood of the new testament and baptismal water.

Jesus is the very Word of God who creates all things. As God spoke in creation, the earth and all things came into being, that is, with the exception of Adam and Eve. The Trinity was there as Adam was formed out of the dust of the ground and God breathed life into him. God caused Adam to fall into a deep sleep. Then, from Adam's side, God brought forth Eve.[91]

---

[91] Genesis 2:7, 21-22.

The apostle Paul often refers to Christ as the second Adam[92] and the church as the bride of Christ.[93] Just as Adam's bride was made from his side, so too the church is born from the side of the second Adam, Christ. We are given life from the side of Christ, the side in which blood and water flowed.

Nothing is made without Christ. In baptism, the Word re-creates us in his own, spotless image. We are united with our Lord and given life from the baptismal waters which flowed from his pierced side. We are reborn as this baptismal river washes away our sins, and unites us with Christ, our life.

Heavenly Father, you have baptized us and placed us into the care of your church. You have given us the gift of your Holy Spirit. Sanctify us as we cling to the promises you have gifted us in baptism. Keep us safe in the ark of Christ and of your church that we may safely reach the shores of the resurrection, where we will finally see the fulfillment of all your promises to us with our own eyes. Amen.

> **FOR FURTHER REFLECTION,
> READ REVELATION 22:1-5.**

---

[92] Romans 5:15-17, 1 Corinthians 15:47-49.
[93] Ephesians 5:25-27.

Baptismal Confidence

NOW WHEN THEY HEARD THIS THEY WERE CUT TO THE HEART, AND SAID TO PETER AND THE REST OF THE APOSTLES, "BROTHERS, WHAT SHALL WE DO?" AND PETER SAID TO THEM, "REPENT AND BE BAPTIZED EVERY ONE OF YOU IN THE NAME OF JESUS CHRIST FOR THE FORGIVENESS OF YOUR SINS, AND YOU WILL RECEIVE THE GIFT OF THE HOLY SPIRIT."

—Acts 2:37-38

Peter never seemed to be at a loss for words. He was often impulsive and always had something to say. At the time of Jesus' transfiguration, it was Peter who was the first to speak up, even though he did not know what he had said.[94] After Jesus' arrest, Peter was not speechless when asked

---

[94] Luke 9:33.

if he knew Jesus. Peter firmly denied his Lord three times ever after asserting, "Even if I must die with you, I will not deny you!" (Matt 26:35).

Although it was Peter who boldly denied his Lord three times, it was also Peter who confidently first proclaimed Jesus to be the Son of God.

> Simon Peter replied, "You are the Christ, the Son of the living God." And Jesus answered him, "Blessed are you, Simon Bar-Jonah! For flesh and blood has not revealed this to you, but my Father who is in heaven" (Matt 16:16-17).

Jesus commends Peter's confession and blesses him. He goes on to state that on this rock, on Peter's confession, he will build his church.[95] Peter speaks up yet again, just a few verses later. But, this time, instead of praise, Peter receives one of the most severe rebukes from the Lord.

> [Jesus] turned and said to Peter, "Get behind me, Satan! You are a hindrance to me. For you are not setting your mind on the things of God, but on the things of man" (Matt 16:23).

Peter wavered. As Jesus foretold Peter's denial, he said to Peter, "I have prayed for you that your faith may not fail" (Luke 22:32). Jesus knew Peter would waiver, but Peter's faith did not fail because Jesus did not fail.

---

[95] Matthew 16:18.

Peter's faith was not dependent upon his actions, thoughts, or feelings. Peter's faith came from outside of himself. Peter's faith *is* Jesus. And, his faith comes as a gift, revealed by his Father who is in heaven.

Fast forward to the day of Pentecost, and Peter spoke up yet again. This time, however, Peter did not deny his Lord or waiver, but boldly proclaimed the gospel. As Peter made his way through the Old Testament Scriptures, he declared the good news of Jesus.

After Peter's sermon, the crowd was cut to the heart. They asked what they must do to be saved. Peter knew not to look inward and direct them to their works or their strength. So, Peter pointed them to where they could receive the One who would never waver.

Peter guided the repentant crowd to the waters of baptism. He directed them to where they would receive the forgiveness of all their sins and the gift of the Holy Spirit.

Our confidence doesn't come from how strongly we feel. Our confidence is in our identity given to us in baptism. It is where Jesus has promised to be for us. Through water and the Word, we receive forgiveness and faith through the working of the Holy Spirit, apart from our works.

We are forgiven and beloved children of our Heavenly Father on account of Christ. Our faith will not fail because Jesus has not failed. Our sin has been buried with Christ. He has conquered our enemies and is risen. Through baptism, we have received the gift of the Holy Spirit who has promised to sustain us in this faith, in Christ.

Heavenly Father, you have baptized us and placed us into the care of your church. You have given us the gift of your Holy Spirit. Sanctify us as we cling to the promises you have gifted us in baptism. Keep us safe in the ark of Christ and of your church that we may safely reach the shores of the resurrection, where we will finally see the fulfillment of all your promises to us with our own eyes. Amen.

> **FOR FURTHER REFLECTION, READ ACTS 2:14-41.**

A Watery Benediction

THE LORD BLESS YOU AND KEEP YOU; THE LORD MAKE HIS FACE TO SHINE UPON YOU AND BE GRACIOUS TO YOU; THE LORD LIFT UP HIS COUNTENANCE UPON YOU AND GIVE YOU PEACE. SO SHALL THEY PUT MY NAME UPON THE PEOPLE OF ISRAEL, AND I WILL BLESS THEM.

—Numbers 6:24-27

In the Old Testament, God is continually putting his name on his people. The Lord is making a promise every time he puts his name on his people. He promises to bless those who bear his holy name and to see to their good. Those marked with the name of the Lord have a God, as the prophet Nehemiah wrote, who is "ready to forgive, gracious and merciful, slow to anger and abounding in steadfast love" (Neh 9:17).

In the book of Exodus, after giving the Ten Commandments to his people, the Lord makes this promise to his people,

"In every place where I cause my name to be remembered I will come to you and bless you" (Exod 20:24).

As the tabernacle is completed, the Lord instructs Aaron and his sons (who are the priests), concerning the blessing.

> The LORD spoke to Moses, saying, "Speak to Aaron and his sons, saying, Thus you shall bless the people of Israel: you shall say to them, The LORD bless you and keep you; the LORD make his face to shine upon you and be gracious to you; the LORD lift up his countenance upon you and give you peace. So shall they put my name upon the people of Israel, and I will bless them" (Num. 6:22-27).

This blessing is unilateral; everything is freely given from God to his people. The blessing requires nothing from his people yet gives everything to them. This is a threefold blessing of gifts and promises from a Triune God who has gifted his name to his people.

In the waters of baptism, we have received a threefold blessing from the Triune God who loves to freely give. In Holy Baptism, we receive this Triune name of God placed upon us. In the Gospel of Matthew, Jesus instructs his disciples on how to place his name on his saints, "Go therefore and make disciples of all nations, baptizing them in the name of the Father and of the Son and of the Holy Spirit" (Matt 28:19).

There is no requirement of works or even faith from us for baptism. There are only gifts freely given from our Lord to us. Our

Lord will see to it that those who bear his name are blessed by the Lord.

As our Great High Priest, Jesus lifted up his hands to bless us. He stretched out his hands to bless us as he hung on the cross for our sin. Jesus, our Great High Priest, blesses us with the forgiveness of all our sins. The Father's face shines upon us even as Jesus is forsaken as he bears our sin.

As we receive God's name in baptism, we receive all our Lord Jesus has won for us. The Lord will bless us and keep us in Christ. The Lord's face shines upon us and is gracious to us as he declares us righteous on account of Christ. Our Heavenly Father's face shines upon us as he makes us his own dear children. We have peace of sins forgiven as we are washed with water and his Word.

Heavenly Father, you have baptized us and placed us into the care of your church. You have given us the gift of your Holy Spirit. Sanctify us as we cling to the promises you have gifted us in baptism. Keep us safe in the ark of Christ and of your church that we may safely reach the shores of the resurrection, where we will finally see the fulfillment of all your promises to us with our own eyes. Amen.

> **FOR FURTHER REFLECTION, READ PSALM 121.**

Appendix

BAPTISMAL PRAYERS

Daily Baptismal Prayer

Heavenly Father, with ordinary water and your Holy Word, you have washed us from our sins and made us your children. Daily put to death in us our old sinful nature. You have forgiven our sin and united us with Christ, our Lord, in the flood of Holy Baptism. There, have called us by name and promised to be with us. Abide with us and keep us in the faith you have graciously given to us through your Holy Spirit. Amen

Morning Baptismal Prayer

Heavenly Father, as we begin the day you have prepared for us, be with us. Remind us this day of all your promises to us as your baptized children. You have placed your name upon us and have promised to go with us. Forgive our sins. Keep us in the baptismal faith you have given to us through your Holy Spirit. Amen.

Evening Baptismal Prayer

Heavenly Father, guard and protect us this evening as we rest from the day's work. In baptism, you have given us the rest and peace of sins forgiven and life everlasting. Forgive our sins and by your Holy Spirit, keep us in this everlasting baptismal rest. You have placed your Holy Name upon us and have promised to be with us always. Comfort us always with your baptismal promises to us through Jesus Christ, our Lord. Amen.

Baptismal Birthday Prayer

Heavenly Father, on this day, you marked me as your own. Through my baptism, you have welcomed me into your family. You have taken my darkness and given me the light of Christ, my Lord. Forgive me when I stray and lead me always back to the still waters of baptism. You have called me by name and have placed your Name upon me that I may cling to your promises, the forgiveness of sins, the resurrection of the body, and life everlasting in Christ. Keep me, by your Holy Spirit, in the faith you have given me in baptism. Amen.

8 BAPTISM QUESTIONS AND ANSWERS

1) Why should I be baptized?

Jesus tells Nicodemus that "unless one is born of water and the Spirit, he cannot enter the kingdom of God" (John 3:5). In the book of Acts, the apostle Peter implores the crowd, "Repent and be baptized every one of you in the name of Jesus Christ for the forgiveness of your sins, and you will receive the gift of the Holy Spirit" (Acts 2:38).

In the gift of baptism, we receive the forgiveness of sins and the gift of the Holy Spirit. We are united with Christ and given new life in baptism (2 Cor 5:17). We are not baptized because it is a work we must do to prove our faith or commitment to Christ, baptism is a gift of life and forgiveness we get to receive!

2) Does it matter how much water?

Jesus said, "Go therefore and make disciples of all nations, baptizing them in the name of the Father and of the Son and of the Holy Spirit, teaching them to observe all that I have commanded you. And behold, I am with you always, to the end of the age" (Matt 28:19-20).

Jesus only commanded us to be baptized in the name of the Father, Son, and Holy Spirit. The Scriptures do not specify how much water, and therefore, we are free to use any amount of water to baptize. The Word is the actor in baptism. Through the Word combined with the water, we receive the forgiveness of sins, life, and salvation. The apostle Peter writes, "you have been born again, not of perishable seed but of imperishable, through the living and abiding word of God" (1 Pet 1:23).

3) Who can be baptized?

The apostle Peter says in the book of Acts, "For the promise is for you and for your children and for all who are far off, everyone whom the Lord our God calls to himself" (Acts 2:39). As Jesus institutes the sacrament of Holy Baptism, he tells his disciples to baptize all nations (Matt 28:19). Jesus rebuked his disciples when they hindered the children from coming to him, saying, "Let the little children come to me and do not hinder them, for to such belongs the kingdom of heaven" (Matt 19:14).

The Scriptures are clear that anyone, regardless of age or nation is to be baptized and receive this gift of forgiveness and union with Christ. Because baptism is God's work and not ours, anyone, regardless of their level of understanding, can receive this gift.

4) Does Jesus alone save or does baptism save me?

Yes! Jesus alone saves, and this salvation is given in the gift of baptism. The apostle Peter writes that baptism now saves you (1 Pet 3:21). The apostle Paul writes in his letter to Titus, "he saved us, not because of works done by us in righteousness, but according to his own mercy, by the washing of regeneration and renewal of the Holy Spirit, whom he poured out on us richly through Jesus Christ our Savior" (Titus 3:5-6). Through baptism, we are saved as we are united with Christ our Redeemer.

5) Do I need to be rebaptized?

The apostle Paul writes, "There is one body and one Spirit—just as you were called to the one hope that belongs to your call—one Lord, one faith, one baptism, one God and Father of all who is over all and through all and in all" (Eph 4:4-5).

Since baptism is God's work alone and not dependent on our faith, work, or understanding, we do not need to be rebaptized. When we are baptized in the name of the Father, Son, and Holy Spirit, we are forgiven, united with Christ, and made Children of God. Our Lord promises as we are baptized, he will be with us always (Matt 28:20). And he keeps his promises.

6) Once I am baptized, can I fall away?

Baptism is an identity. We are baptized! We can fall away through daily sin and act as if we aren't baptized. But, through the working of the Holy Spirit, we are also repented and turned back to the promises given in our baptism. We are reminded by the apostle Paul that in baptism God "saved us, not because of works done by us in righteousness, but according to his own mercy" (Titus 3:5).

7) What if I doubt?

When we have doubts, we cry out in prayer to our Heavenly Father as the father in Mark's Gospel, "I believe; help my unbelief!" (Mark 9:24).

In baptism, we receive the gift of the Holy Spirit (Acts 2:38). The apostle Paul writes, "you have received the Spirit of adoption as sons, by whom we cry, Abba! Father! The Spirit himself bears witness with our spirit that we are children of God" (Rom 8:15-16). When doubts may come, we look to the name into which we have been baptized. We have been baptized in the name of our Heavenly Father, the Son of God who has redeemed us, and the Holy Spirit who has been gifted to us to testify of these truths.

8) How do I know that I am saved? How can I be sure?

Baptism unites us to the death and resurrection of Jesus. The apostle Paul writes, "Do you not know that all of us who have been baptized into Christ Jesus were baptized into his death? We were buried therefore with him by baptism into death in order that, just as Christ was raised from the dead by the glory of the Father, we too might walk in newness of life" (Rom 6:3-4).

We can be certain of our salvation and forgiveness because we are baptized into Christ! We are marked with water and the resurrected Word. Our Lord has taken our sin away in his death and has wrapped us up in his righteousness. We are forgiven and to be certain and for our comfort, our Lord gave us this blessed gift of Holy Baptism.

More Best Sellers from

Find these titles
and more at 1517.org/shop

1517.

Never Go Another Day Without Hearing the Gospel of Jesus.

Visit **www.1517.org**
for free Gospel resources.

www.ingramcontent.com/pod-product-compliance
Lightning Source LLC
LaVergne TN
LVHW041333080426
835512LV00006B/435